Adam

Adam

God's Beloved

HENRI J.M. NOUWEN

DARTON · LONGMAN + TODD

First published by Orbis Books in 1997

First published in Great Britain in 1997 by
Darton, Longman and Todd Ltd
1 Spencer Court
140–142 Wandsworth High Street
London SW18 4JJ

Reprinted 2000, 2001, 2009, 2010, 2013, 2014, 2015, 2017

ISBN 0–232–52246–4

A catalogue record for this book is available
from the British Library

Designed by Sandie Boccacci
Phototypeset in 11/15½pt Galliard by Intype London Ltd
Printed and bound in Great Britain by
Bell and Bain Ltd, Glasgow

To
Jeanne and Rex Arnett

❦

Contents

Foreword by Sue Mosteller CSJ   ix

Introduction – How This Book Came
to Be Written   1

1. Adam's Hidden Life   7

2. Adam's Desert   21

3. Adam's Public Life   28

4. Adam's Way   54

5. Adam's Passion   70

6. Adam's Death   78

7. Adam's Wake and Burial   90

8. Adam's Resurrection   102

9. Adam's Spirit   108

    Conclusion   112

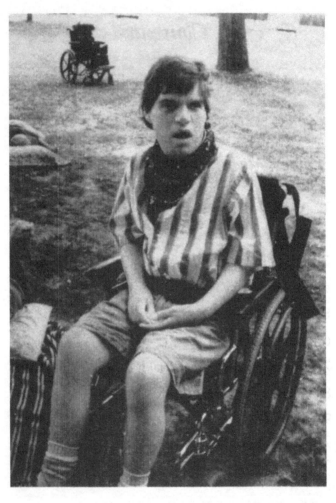

Adam Arnett
(1961–1996)

❦

Foreword

VERY SHORTLY AFTER Adam Arnett died in February 1996, Henri told me that he was thinking of writing a book about Adam. He wanted to do it, and he wanted to know if I could help him by telling him stories about Adam's life. I was shocked, because for me it was too soon after Adam's death to be writing a book. I told him I needed more time. That was hard for Henri. And so he wrote the book without me. That was hard for me!

He sent a first draft to his publisher, Robert Ellsberg, and they corresponded about the strong and weak points in the manuscript and about the work that needed to be done. Henri also talked to Jeanne and Rex Arnett, Adam's parents, asking for time to hear stories and facts about Adam's early life. They planned to get together so Henri would have more material for the first two chapters.

Then Henri died suddenly on 21 September 1996.

Named literary executrix in Henri's will, I inherited

among other things the responsibility for the completion of this book. I was supported by Henri's publisher, and I visited Adam's parents. Then I began to work on the manuscript.

What struck me initially was the power and the significance of this relationship between Adam and Henri. It happened at a particular moment in Henri's life when he was searching for home. Adam, by his simplicity and by his presence, welcomed Henri home. It is an incredible story.

I was also aware of the weakness in the text, especially with respect to Adam's early life, so I worked to strengthen that section. Doing it allowed me to grieve the loss of my two good friends. I talked to them while I worked, but I didn't ever 'hear' them responding. However, I was greatly energised in the process, and I worked with passion and conviction. That, for me, was their presence and guiding spirit. I do believe they helped me.

The text, describing their relationship, has inspired me deeply, in the midst of my own sorrow. I'm very grateful now that Henri took the initiative, and I'm thankful to have been given the opportunity to contribute to Adam and Henri's story. Like Henri, I did it with love, with great joy, and with freedom.

Henri patterns Adam's story after the life of Jesus, and he does it beautifully. Not only that, but he realises in the writing that Adam's story is his own story. Finally, by his genius as a writer, Henri gifts each of us with our stories as well.

Sue Mosteller CSJ
Henri Nouwen Literary Centre
L'Arche Daybreak
Richmond Hill, Ontario

1 May 1997

☙

How This Book Came to Be Written

BEGINNING IN SEPTEMBER 1995, the people of L'Arche Daybreak offered me a sabbatical to celebrate my ten years as their pastor. Because my deepest desire was to write, I chose to spend the year working on several themes that have inspired and supported me in my ministry. Many of these thoughts were shaped by my life in the community of Daybreak, which has become a true home for me.

I had been pondering, 'What do I believe?' 'What does it mean when I say that I believe in God: Father, Son, and Holy Spirit?' 'What do I say when I recite the articles of faith?' These questions had been with me for quite a while so I decided to write a small book about the Apostles' Creed.

I spoke about it with several people and proposed to my friend and publisher, Robert Ellsberg, that I start working on a contemporary confession of faith. Although I was primarily concerned to find a new way to express the faith that I have tried to live all of my life, I also believed that this would help the many men and women in our world who are struggling with the same questions and for whom the traditional formulas have lost their meaning and relevance.

Robert Ellsberg was quite excited about the idea and took the time and energy to collect a series of articles about the Creed. As I started to read them I soon found myself immersed in very complicated theological discussions about the origins and various forms of the central formulation of the faith of the Christian. I began to wonder if my seemingly simple plan wasn't going to be in fact an ambitious and pretentious undertaking. I simply desired to express in understandable language how we can live our lives in the name of our loving God. The more I read the less easy it seemed. I had to ask myself how I dared to write a responsible book about the Creed of all Christians, having left the academic life more than a decade ago and having no intention of doing deep theological research. Wasn't I now primarily a pastor of a small community with people who have mental disabilities? Surely that is not the most obvious context in which to discuss the twelve articles of our faith. Most of the people I live with in the community of Daybreak never articulate their beliefs systematically, and for many of them reflective thinking on theological articles is difficult if not impossible.

Just as I started to wonder if I wasn't trying to reach far beyond my limits, Adam Arnett died. Adam was my friend, my teacher, and my guide: an unusual friend, because he couldn't express affection and love in the way most people do; an unusual teacher, because he couldn't think reflectively or articulate ideas or concepts; an unusual guide, because he couldn't give me any concrete direction or advice. Adam was one of my housemates when I first came to L'Arche Daybreak. He was the first person I was asked to care for when I joined the L'Arche Daybreak community in Toronto where he lived.

From the moment I saw Adam's body lying in his casket, I was struck by the mystery of this man's life and death. In a flash I knew in my heart that this very disabled human being was loved by God from all eternity and sent into the world with a unique mission of healing, which was now fulfilled. I recognised many parallels between the story of Jesus and the story of Adam. And I knew something else. I knew, in a very profound place, that Adam, in some mysterious way, had become an image of the living Christ for me just as Jesus, when he lived on the earth, was friend, teacher, and guide for his disciples. In and through Adam I came to a truly new understanding of those relationships of Jesus, not just as they were lived long ago, but as Jesus desires to live them now, with me and with us, through the weakest and most vulnerable people. Indeed, not only did I come to know more about God by caring for Adam, but also Adam helped me, by his life, to discover and rediscover the Spirit of Jesus alive in my own 'poorness of spirit'. Jesus lived long ago, but Adam lived in my time. Jesus was physically present to his disciples. Adam was physically present to me. Jesus was Emmanuel, God with us. Adam became for me a sacred person, a holy man, an image of the living God.

Was Adam very unusual? Was he some special angel? Not at all. Adam was one person among many others. But I had a relationship with Adam, and he became special for me. I loved him, and our relationship was one of the most significant of my life. Adam's death touched me deeply because for me he was the one who more than any book or professor led me to the person of Jesus. His death was a wake-up call. It seemed as if he said to me, 'Now that I have left you, you can write about me and tell your friends and readers what I have taught you about the mystery of our wonderful God who came to dwell among us and who sent us the Holy Spirit.'

❦

When, after Adam's burial, I returned to my writing, I was facing once again my question: 'What do I believe?' Then I became aware that this was a question that Adam could help me to answer. I stopped reading my theological and historical articles and began to ponder the life and vocation of this remarkable man who died at about the same age as Jesus, 34. As I let his short life pass through my mind and heart I realised that Adam's life story would give me words to speak about my faith and about the Christian Creed in a way that people could easily understand. Adam, who never spoke a word, gradually became a true source of words for me to express my deepest conviction as a Christian, living at the turn of the second millennium. He who was so vulnerable became a powerful support to help me announce the richness of Christ. And he who could not expressly recognise me, would, through me, help others recognise God in their lives.

Adam's unexpected death and my own grief led me to the interior place I had been searching for where I was able to speak about God and God's entering into human history. I realised that his story would help me to tell Jesus' story, because Jesus' story had helped me to understand Adam's story.

He could have been called John or Peter. The fact that he who revealed Jesus to me in a very special way was called Adam was purely coincidental, but a coincidence that was also providential. Like the first Adam, our Adam represents every human person and thus more easily raises the question: 'Who is your Adam who speaks to you about God?'

I started to write, and the story that follows is probably as close as I will ever come to writing about the Apostles' Creed. Adam is the door to the expression of this Creed, so I write with love and gratitude for him and for our special relationship. I also write with the deep hope that many others, through Adam's story, will be enabled to recognise God's story among us and so be empowered to say in a new way, 'I do believe.'

❦

CHAPTER ONE

Adam's Hidden Life

ADAM WAS THE second son of Jeanne and Rex Arnett, born on 17 November 1961. He was a beautiful baby who brought so much life and energy to his parents, his eight-year-old brother, Michael, and his grandparents. Because Michael suffered from frequent epileptic seizures and needed constant assistance, Jeanne and Rex requested that Adam be thoroughly tested for epilepsy. All the tests proved negative, and that was a big relief.

But Adam was slow to nurse, which worried his mother. When he was three months old he developed a serious ear infection accompanied by a high fever. Jeanne recognised his first seizure immediately; she wrapped him in a blanket and took him next door to her neighbour, a nurse, who drove them to the hospital. Later that night the doctor confirmed that Adam too was epileptic.

Adam took his time learning to crawl, and he was more than a year old before he stood. Then, for a long time he walked in the house holding onto the furniture, moving slowly, carefully, and safely around it. Finally, one day when he was two years old, he let go and walked without support. His parents were delighted.

Seizures followed, and medication was prescribed, but basically Adam had several years when he was physically quite well. He never learned to speak, but he followed instructions, knew what was happening around him, and communicated in his own way. When his father made a buzzing noise and circled with his finger above Adam's head until the 'bee' gently landed on Adam's nose, he would grab his father's arm and make a circle in the air to indicate that he wanted to play that game again.

By the time he was four, he had certain patterns of getting around and especially liked to go out behind the house where he climbed on the picnic table and sat, waiting for his mother to bring him some juice. Then he would go to the end of the table, where there was no bench, and begin the descent. But when he got his feet over the edge, he hung there, going neither up nor down. He didn't say anything, but simply waited to be rescued. He had been taught how to get down, but he liked this way better. Quietly, he waited for help to come. This simple posture of waiting, begun so early, was the dominant character-istic of his life.

Because Adam could neither play nor speak like other children his age, he did not have the opportunity to develop friendships or to expand his horizons. Apart from his family, Adam's life and development were less celebrated and more seen in relationship to his disabilities.

Adam also liked to walk out from behind the house, down the street and back. Even though four houses on the street looked the same, he always knew which one was his and would not go beyond it. When he ran, he plodded down the street with his arms up in the air. Sometimes the neighbours recognised him and called to alert his parents, fearing that he was on the move.

After he outgrew the children's seat in the shopping trolley, Jeanne still had to take him with her to shop, so she sat him in the trolley and put the shopping on top of him. 'He was very quiet when we started,' Jeanne recalls, 'but when I was looking for things, he would reach out and put things into the trolley. I would scold him and say that I did not want that, but he never gave up trying. At the beginning he sat quietly, but as the shopping piled in on top of him, he fussed and moved things around. I had to reassure him that we were almost finished and that he would be free in a few minutes. As the trolley got full he would lift up one item after another and slowly and quietly put his arm out over the edge and let go. Because of Adam, I sometimes came home with more than I wanted and other times I came home with less!' But in the midst of it all Rex and Jeanne kept their sense of humour.

Adam loved to eat, especially puddings. Often, since Michael was very talkative and not attentive to his food, Adam would reach over and get his spoon into Michael's pudding. Sometimes he would even try to pull Michael's plate towards him when Michael wasn't looking. Rex and Jeanne enjoyed Adam's little vices.

The utility cupboard in the Arnetts' home was located at the top of the staircase on a landing. One day Rex noticed that Adam had opened the door and pulled out the vacuum cleaner. Adam was fascinated as he discovered that he could move it little by little to the edge of the long staircase in front of him. Rex says: 'I was at the bottom of the stairs and excited to see him initiating something, so I called Jeanne to come and watch with me. Adam kept throwing glances at us every time he pulled the Hoover closer to the edge of the stairs, somehow knowing that he was doing something mischievous. Finally he gave it a great push, and down it came, crashing on each step as it fell.' Rex tells this story as a little victory. Adam had done something! Something with a bang! Rex was so thrilled that he told Adam, 'Do it again!' And in telling the story Rex laughingly concludes, 'We were willing to buy an extra Hoover just for him to keep throwing it down the stairs so he would experience his power.'

Adam didn't meet the criteria for school, which added to his childhood isolation. When he was 8-years-old Jeanne found a group of parents who ran, with volunteers, a small group for disabled children, which Adam was able to attend for two hours a day. He was finally able to go to school when he was ten years old, but he often arrived late or had to be picked up early because of his seizures. His academic life was limited as was his social life. Adam was not invited to many birthday parties and for most of his childhood he was hidden in his home with his immediate family.

He did however take a liking to sports. Soon after beginning at the school, Adam started to jump up and down on his bed at all times of the day and night. His parents loved it whenever Adam did anything on his own. But this was dangerous, and they were worried about his safety, so they tried hard to help him see that this was not the best place to jump. He thought it was! Rex strengthened the bed, which needed constant repairing, but one day the whole thing collapsed. It was soon after that incident that the school showed the parents a poorly made video of one of the students bouncing up and down on the trampoline. Jeanne asked whose child it was, and the teacher answered, 'Yours!' That solved the mystery.

Adam was not fully recognised in his church and it was painful for his parents when they learned that because of his handicap Adam could not receive the sacraments of Eucharist and Confirmation with the other children of his age. Later though, in a small faith-sharing group, Adam made his First Communion and celebrated with this small community of friends.

❦

During his hidden years, Adam was communicating in his own unique ways, but he wasn't always very well understood. There was one difficult year for Adam when he was diagnosed as being deaf. He was tested by specialists and fitted with hearing aids, which he disliked enormously. For months, no matter how hard people tried to help him adapt and accept these devices, he showed his discomfort and did everything to rip them from his ears. Only after almost a year had passed did a second diagnosis reveal that he was not deaf and that the hearing aids were amplifying the sound he could already hear, which was hurting his ears. Adam's father remarks, 'I think he suffered so much, but we never knew because he could not tell us.'

Adam was unable to tell the time, but he knew about meal-times. Every day at 5 p.m. he went to the kitchen, slowly opened the sliding cupboard doors, took out a saucepan, and placed it on the cooker. This was to remind Jeanne that it was time to begin getting supper. If Jeanne didn't take the hint, he shook the saucepan and made certain that she 'heard' that supper was the next priority.

When Adam was 13 years old he went for a two-week session on toilet training in a centre for people with disabilities. He had two characteristics that the staff at the centre knew nothing about: he loved to eat, and he urinated only when he was wearing a nappy or his jockey shorts. While staff were amazed and delighted that he was the only one there who was able to find the dining room on his own, they could not grasp why, after three or four hours sitting on the toilet with no result, once he had his shorts back on he became Niagara Falls! When the training was over, Rex picked him up in his brand new car. It must have followed a long afternoon of training because as soon as Adam got into the car, it was quickly 'baptized'. Adam was smiling.

❦

A short time later on a day when his father was away at a sales meeting, Jeanne was home with the boys. As she went upstairs to get something, she said to Michael, 'Keep an eye on your brother for a moment and I'll be right back.' While she was upstairs the phone rang, and as she was talking on the phone, Michael began to scream, 'Come! Come! Emergency! Emergency!' Jeanne ran down the stairs to find Adam lying against the couch in so much blood that she was unable to find the source. When she lifted his head she saw in her terror that because of his fall his two front teeth had been pushed up into his gums.

13

At the hospital, he had surgery to have his teeth put back into place with caps on them. The doctors said that during the seizure and the fall Adam had cut a 'V' out of his tongue, and that was the source of all the blood.

This seizure changed Adam's life. The doctors at the hospital gave him a thorough check and decided to prescribe new medication. In the days following, his mother kept telling the nurses that the boy lying immobilised on the bed was not like the boy who lived in her home, walked about by himself, and participated in the life of the household. She was told there was nothing more they could do, and she could take him home. After three more days at home, she called a Public Health nurse, who was able to unravel the mystery. The doctors, after making out the new prescription, had failed to cancel the old medication so that Adam was overdosed for several days. As a result there was permanent damage, and Adam was never the same after this experience. He had very little energy, and he had lost a lot of his ability to get around and to direct his own activity. He needed help to walk and often had to be carried. His seizures were frequent and draining. When he wasn't feeling too well, with an upset stomach or other discomfort, he would find his mother or father and cuddle quietly against them in a gentle embrace. He loved this position and could rest content for long periods of time.

When I ask Rex about Adam he says, 'Adam was

our peacemaker. By his quiet presence he always brought us again to a still place in ourselves and created a loving atmosphere in our home.' Rex does not say much about the enormous work that caring for Michael and Adam required of him and Jeanne. Lifting, bathing, shaving, feeding, laundry, dressing and undressing, schools and day programmes, doctors and specialists – it was a huge task.

When Jeanne was diagnosed with dangerously high blood pressure, she was advised to begin looking for long-term placements for Michael and Adam in facilities that care for people with disabilities. This was an unthinkable sentence for Rex and Jeanne as parents, but they also knew that it was impossible to keep the boys at home for the long-term. Adam and Michael were becoming young men, and their care was a major undertaking. It was time for them to find new surroundings. But where should they go?

Their parents knew about L'Arche Daybreak because several people from that community were part of their small faith group. L'Arche is an international federation of communities, based on the Beatitudes and founded by the Canadian Jean Vanier in 1964. Each community consists of homes in ordinary neighbourhoods where folks with disabilities and their assistants live together, sharing life in a spirit of mutuality. L'Arche believes that 'people with a mental handicap often possess qualities of welcome, wonderment, spontaneity, and directness' and that

15

'they are a living reminder to the wider world of the essential values of the heart' (Charter of L'Arche).

The Arnetts had visited Daybreak on several occasions. Even though they knew the people were good people, they found it hard to imagine placing their children in the midst of that inexperienced group of young assistants. As parents, they saw that there was much love and care, but it was a large group of people, and there was a casual attitude in the group. Michael and Adam's parents were frightened that the needs of their sons might be compromised. They did inquire seriously however, only to be told that to date the community had never welcomed anyone with epilepsy or with any special medical needs, that it wasn't equipped at that time to welcome a member with as many needs as Adam, but that Michael could be a candidate because he was able to walk and to provide some of his own self-care.

A long and painful search ensued, during which these beautiful parents visited many agencies and institutions. They were shocked and astonished to see the condition of some of the available placements for Adam, where people had to live in smelly, dreary, and lonely conditions. Rex says it was the first time, in all those years, that he experienced hopelessness.

They went back to Daybreak. When a place became available, Michael, very reluctantly, moved into the Daybreak 'Green House'. Later, Adam was placed in a chronic care hospital close to his parents' home.

They could visit him every day, which they did for the next five years.

These transition years were like a long purgatory for Rex and Jeanne, not to mention Michael and Adam. Michael, very sad at losing the comfort and care of his family, was initially unhappy at Daybreak and pleaded to return home to regain all that he had lost. Adam, in the impersonal environment of a hospital ward with others in need of long-term care, responded by losing weight, as well as his ability to stand, walk, or move around on his own. It was heartbreaking for Rex and Jeanne, whose very identity had been shaped by their relationship with their two sons. Now they had to let them go into the care of others who did not know them and who could never provide the same love and attention which they had given. They continually questioned, 'Is there any other way to do this?' 'Could Adam ever have a home?'

❦

As I think about this first part of Adam's life I cannot avoid seeing a close parallel with Jesus' home life. Jesus did not come in power and might. He came dressed in weakness. The greatest part of his life was hidden, sharing the human condition as a baby, a young child, a struggling adolescent, and a maturing adult. Adam's hidden life, like the life of Jesus in Nazareth, was an unseen preparation for the time of his ministry to many people, even though neither he nor his parents looked on it that way.

I am not saying that Adam was a second Jesus. But I am saying that because of the vulnerability of Jesus we can see Adam's extremely vulnerable life as a life of utmost spiritual significance. Adam did not have unique heroic virtues: he did not excel in anything that newspapers write about. But I am convinced that Adam was chosen to witness to God's love through his brokenness. To say this is not to romanticise him or to be sentimental. Adam was, like all of us, a limited person, more limited than most, and unable to express himself in words. But he was also a whole person and a blessed man. In his weakness he became a unique instrument of God's grace. He became a revelation of Christ among us.

Adam possessed an inner light that was radiant. It was of God. He had few distractions, few attachments, and few ambitions to fill his inner space. Therefore Adam did not have to practice the spiritual disciplines to become empty for God. His so-called 'disability' gifted him with it. For him God was never the subject of an intellectual or emotional search. Like Jesus, his belovedness, his likeness to God, his mission of peace could be acknowledged only by those who were willing to welcome him as one sent by God.

Most people saw Adam as a disabled person who had little to give and who was a burden to his family, his community, and to society at large. And as long

18

as he was seen that way, his truth was hidden. What was not received was not given.

But Adam's parents loved him simply because he was Adam. Yes, they recognised and loved him for himself. Without awareness they also welcomed him as one sent to us by God in utter vulnerability to be an instrument of God's blessing. That vision of him changes everything quite radically because then Adam emerges as someone, as special, as a wonderful, gifted, child of promise.

His transparency would later enable us, at Daybreak and beyond, to recognise something of God's unconditional love. His wonderful presence and his incredible worth would enlighten us to comprehend that we, like him, are also precious, graced, and beloved children of God, whether we see ourselves as rich or poor, intelligent or disabled, good-looking or unattractive. As a spiritual teacher he would lead us ever so gently to those inner spaces we prefer to leave untouched, so that each of us could live out our true vocations. In relationship with him we would discover a deeper, truer identity.

But all that promise was hidden in his early life. I don't think Adam's parents spoke or thought about their son in this perspective. Nor, I think, did the parents of Jesus. But that doesn't exclude this understanding of the mystery of his life which gradually emerged after his death. That is what happened to Jesus. That is what happened to Adam. That is what

19

has happened to most people we consider as history's great spiritual guides.

In God's eyes the most significant is often the most hidden. The stories about Adam's 18 years at home with his parents are very ordinary. They are not about miracles or unusual happenings. They are about a small family living in their suburban home, trying hard to live a normal life with two wonderful, not-so-normal boys. They are about Adam, whose beauty remained mysteriously veiled to all those he met with the exception of his family and a few 'enlightened' friends.

CHAPTER TWO

❧

Adam's Desert

THE GOSPELS TELL US that just after his baptism, Jesus was led by the Spirit into the wilderness for forty days where he was tempted by the devil. The desert, in the spiritual life, is the place of temptation, trial, and purification. Adam also lived a 'wilderness' time.

The chronic care hospital, because of government policy, refused to take Adam until he was 18 years of age and eligible for a government disability pension. When his first cheque arrived, Jeanne took it to the hospital. They accepted it and opened a bed for Adam.

Jeanne and Rex were introduced to Adam's roommates on his first day in the hospital: an 80-year-old stroke patient who was bed-ridden and unable to communicate, a gentle man suffering from multiple sclerosis, and a young Jamaican paralysed because of a broken neck suffered in a work-related accident. The room was large with two big windows. Adam's bed was close to the door.

The following day when his mother came for an afternoon visit, she found Adam, up and dressed, sitting silently but tied, hand, waist, and foot, to his wheel-chair. In a state of shock, disbelief, anger, and sadness, she told the staff that Adam was truly not going anywhere and that the restraints were not needed. In time they got to know Adam and his needs.

The hospital was understaffed so there was little presence and no programmes to take patients out of their rooms or to offer them stimulation of mind or body. Physical attention was given on schedule, trays were delivered, but life was dull, boring, and lonely.

Within a short time his parents had taken on the responsibility of feeding Adam his noon and evening meals. Friends were invited to or offered to come and feed Adam when his parents couldn't be there. This provided Adam with visits, conversation, and special treats which only those who knew him could give.

In the five years that Adam lived his desert experience, he never spoke his feelings and thoughts about his life in the hospital. He couldn't protest or rally for a better life; he couldn't even show his loneliness, his pain, or his discontent. For many hours in the days and in the nights he was alone and silent, patiently waiting for a home.

Regularly Adam came home for the weekend. Rex comments, 'He was such a gentle soul, and we loved to have him with us.' While they tried desperately to make life as comfortable as possible for Adam, the main concern for Jeanne and Rex was to find Adam a place that could be his home. They continued their search. They visited homes, agencies, and institutions in all parts of Ontario, seeking a placement suitable for Adam.

One day Rex discovered that Adam had once again had a seizure and hit his chin, forcing his front teeth up into his gums. No one had noticed that it had happened so he did not know how long Adam had been waiting for treatment and relief. When Rex asked for help, he was told that there were no dentists on the staff and that he would have to take Adam to see his own dentist. This time Adam lost his two front teeth.

Rex and Jeanne got close to Adam's roommate Peter. Peter sometimes looked rather frightening because his hair was thick, black, and bushy, but in fact, he was a most patient and gentle man. He became, in a way, a spokesperson for Adam. When Jeanne and Rex came, he could tell them that Adam had had a bad night, that Adam had had no seizures that day, or that certain friends of Adam's had been in to visit. Peter had friends from the Jamaican community in Toronto who often visited him, but the visit he cherished most was that of his mother. She came on the bus from New York once a month bringing a bit of 'home', with her love and her

Jamaican food for Peter. Peter also loved Rex, Jeanne, Adam, and their friends, who talked with him and helped him to pass his long and lonely days.

❦

Adam's time in the hospital was without doubt his desert. Just as God's Spirit overshadowed Jesus in the Jordan and then drove him to the desert, that same Spirit overshadowed Adam during his time at home and drove him to this place of purification. It was a time of temptation, maybe not so much for Adam himself as for those who had seen in him a gift and had called him 'our peacemaker'. They were discouraged in their search and by the definition that our society gives to marginal people. Who was there to recognise this beautiful man of God in a place that is large, anonymous, routinely run, and understaffed? Who could acknowledge Adam's uniqueness in a context where he and all his fellow 'patients' were approached not so much as human beings but as objects of care? Who could celebrate Adam's life when there was hardly time to give him a bath and feed him? There was pressure to forget Adam's divine origin and sacred mission.

Adam was sent to bring Good News to the world. It was his mission, as it was the mission of Jesus. Adam was – very simply, quietly, and uniquely – there! He was a person, who by his very life announced the marvellous mystery of our God: I am precious, beloved, whole, and born of God. Adam bore silent witness to this mystery which has nothing to do with whether or not he could speak, walk, or express himself, whether or not he made money, had a job, was fashionable, famous, married or single. It had to do with his being. He was and is a beloved child of God. It is the same news that Jesus came to announce, and it is the news that all those who are poor keep proclaiming in and through their very weakness. Life is a gift. Each one of us is unique, known by name, and loved by the One who fashioned us. Unfortunately, there is a very loud, consistent, and powerful message coming to us from our world that leads us to believe that we must prove our belovedness by how we look, by what we have, and by what we can accomplish. We become preoccupied with 'making it' in this life, and we are very slow to grasp the liberating truth of our origins and our finality. We need to hear the message announced and see the message embodied, over and over again. Only then do we find the courage to claim it and to live from it.

Jesus didn't accomplish much during his lifetime. He died as a failure. Adam didn't accomplish much either. He died as poor as he was born. Still, both Jesus and Adam are God's beloved sons – Jesus by nature, Adam by 'adoption' – and they lived their sonship among us as the only thing that they had to offer. That was their assigned mission. That is also my mission and yours. Believing it and living from it is true sanctity.

❧

These years in the hospital were the concluding years of Adam's hidden life. In so many ways Adam was only a 'client' to most of the professional teachers, doctors, nurses, dentists, social workers, ministers and government employees who met him, worked with him, and yet failed to recognise or receive his beautiful spirit, his enduring patience, and his gentle heart.

But Rex, Jeanne, and their friends kept Adam's truth alive. They overcame the temptation to look only at Adam's disabilities. Indeed they accepted that he couldn't change stones into bread, or jump safely from a high tower, or acquire great wealth, but he didn't have to do any of these worldly things because they knew his belovedness deep in their hearts. This divine knowledge made them look for more than five years for a home for Adam, a place where he could manifest his gifts and exercise his unique ministry.

Daybreak wasn't equipped to welcome Adam because of his physical and medical needs. But, with time, friendship was blossoming between the parents and the people of Daybreak. The community that had welcomed Michael as one of its core members also came to see Rex, Jeanne, and Adam's great sorrow. Gradually it became clear that Adam should be with his brother at Daybreak and that all the arrangements to allow this to happen needed to be made.

Daybreak's preparation was long. One of the assistants was sent to L'Arche in France to become acquainted with caring for people with greater physical and medical needs. A section of the New House was renovated with a special bathroom, railings along the walls, and wheelchair accessibility. A special day programme was initiated to provide daytime activities for core members in the wider community of Richmond Hill. It took more than a year, but finally everything was in place to welcome Adam to his new home. There was hope for Rex and Jeanne! There was joy for Michael, who had been waiting all these years to live with his brother. There was expectation, some fear, and much excitement for all the people in Daybreak as they welcomed Michael's brother and expanded its mission to include someone with greater needs.

On 1 May 1985, Rex and Jeanne helped to move their second son to the New House at Daybreak. Michael was on hand and full of joy. Jeanne cried as she arranged furniture and clothing in his new room. Rex joked with the assistants as they unloaded Adam's belongings. His public life was beginning.

❦

CHAPTER THREE

Adam's Public Life

IN AUGUST 1986 I met Adam for the first time. Upon arrival at Daybreak I was given a basement bedroom in the New House, one of the eight homes of the community. This home and the people who lived there were to become my primary place of belonging within the larger body of Daybreak. Here I could get to know the daily life of a normal L'Arche home.

Besides Adam I met other housemates: Roy, 75 years old, who had lived for 50 years in a large institution for people with disabilities; John, with Down's syndrome, who was in his thirties; Rosie, who had spent 20 of her 22 years in a nursing home; and Michael, in his early twenties, who had no contact with his family and who suffered from severe cerebral palsy. These disabled persons are called 'core members' at Daybreak because they are at the heart of the community life that forms around them. The assistants in the home were young men and women from several different countries who had come to spend a year or more living with and creating a home with the core members in the New House.

I was told that L'Arche's mission was to 'live with' core members, so I embarked on my new life with all the people in the New House. Manual work, cooking and housekeeping skills were alien to me. I had been teaching for 20 years at universities in Holland and the United States, and during this time I had never given much attention to creating a home nor had I been close to people with disabilities. In my family and among my friends, I had earned a reputation for being impractical, and my friends often call me 'the absent-minded professor'.

But, absent-minded or not, I was soon asked the question, 'Henri, would you help Adam in the morning to get ready for his day? It means doing his morning routine.' Helping Adam meant waking him up at 7 a.m., taking off his pyjamas and dressing him in a bathrobe, walking him to the bathroom, shaving his beard, giving him a bath, choosing clothes for the day, dressing him, combing his hair, walking with him to the kitchen, making his breakfast, sitting close beside him as he ate his breakfast, supporting his glass as he drank, brushing his teeth, putting on his coat, gloves, and cap, getting him into his wheelchair, and pushing him over the pothole-rich road to his Daybreak day programme, where he would spend the day until 4 p.m.

I was aghast! I simply didn't think I could do this.

'What if he falls? How do I support him as he walks? What if I hurt him and he cannot even tell me? What if he has a seizure? What if I make his bath too hot or too cold? What if I cut him? I do not even know how to dress him! So many things can go wrong. Besides, I don't know the man. I'm not a nurse. I have no training in this kind of thing!' Some of these many objections I voiced; most of them I just thought. But the answer was clear, firm, and reassuring: 'You can do it. First of all we will help you and give you plenty of time until you feel comfortable. when you feel ready you can do it all alone. Even then you have only to call us when you have a question. It will take a while, but you will catch on. You'll learn the routine, and you will get to know Adam and he will get to know you.'

So I began with fear and trembling. I still remember those first days. Even with the support of other assistants, I was afraid walking into Adam's room and waking up this stranger. His heavy breathing and restless hand movements made me very self-conscious. I didn't know him. I didn't know what he expected of me. I didn't want to upset him. And in front of the others, I didn't want to make a fool of myself. I didn't want to be laughed at. I didn't want to be a source of embarrassment.

At first, not knowing how to relate to Adam without talking and exchanging as I did with others, I concentrated on the routine. In those early days I saw him as someone who was *very* different from me. I did not have any expectation that we would communicate because he did not talk. The frequent interruptions of his breathing by moments of silence made me wonder if he would be able to take a next breath. He sometimes flailed with his hands, and he intertwined his fingers in and out, which made me think something was bothering him, but I had no idea what that might be. When I walked with him I had to get behind him and support him with my body and my arms. I worried constantly that he would trip on my feet, fall and hurt himself. I was also conscious that he could have a grand mal seizure at any moment: sitting in the bath, on the toilet, eating his breakfast, resting, walking, or being shaved.

At first I had to keep asking myself and others, 'Why have you asked me to do this? Why did I say yes? What am I doing here? Who is this stranger who is demanding such a big chunk of my time each day? Why should I, the least capable of all the people in the house, be asked to take care of Adam and not of someone whose needs are a bit less?' The answer was always the same: 'So you can get to know Adam.' Now that was a puzzle for me. Adam often looked at me and followed me with his eyes, but he did not speak or respond to anything I asked him. Adam didn't smile when I did something well or protest when I made a mistake. I wondered if he even recognised me. How would I get to know him? What, I asked myself, was he thinking, was he feeling, was he sensing? What was his experience with me?

During the first few weeks I kept calling from the bathroom: 'Please help me. Please come and give me a hand. I can't get him in the tub. I can't find his toothbrush. I don't know if these are his work trousers or his dress trousers. Please stay with him while I get his razor. I don't dare to leave him alone.' They always came: Anneika, Regina, D.J., Steve, or anyone who happened to be close by. 'Keep at it, Henri,' they kept telling me. 'You're just getting to know him. Pretty soon you'll be an old hand! Pretty soon you'll love him.' I had so much anxiety that I could not imagine what 'loving Adam' would mean.

As much as I tried, it just didn't make much sense to me. Aren't you supposed to have the best-trained people working with the most disabled ones? Don't you assign the best for the neediest? But the assistants kept telling me that here we do not see ourselves as caregivers and patients, or as staff and clients. Some of us are assistants and some are core members. Each one – yes, each person – is indeed, an amateur, which literally means 'a lover'.

But I was not conscious of that in the beginning. For a while all my attention went on doing the right things and making as few mistakes as possible. By doing that I finally learned the routine, and I began to gain confidence in myself. I have no idea whether Adam had confidence in me or not.

It usually took me two hours to get Adam up and out of his bedroom into the bathroom, out of the bathroom into the kitchen, out of the kitchen into his wheelchair, and off to his day programme. When I had finally delivered him there, I felt a deep sense of relief and went to work, doing what I can do well: talking, dictating letters, counselling, making phone calls, leading meetings, giving sermons, presiding over ceremonies. That was the world where I felt at ease and capable.

Still, I have to say that, from the very beginning, there was for me, a sense of privilege. I felt grateful that the young assistants of the New House kept encouraging me to help Adam and kept showing me that I could do it. I felt grateful that I was not excused as being too old, too clumsy, or too inexperienced to give it a try. But most of all I felt particularly honoured that the weakest and most disabled man of the house – yes, of the whole community – was entrusted to me. At some level I knew that this was what L'Arche is all about: placing the weakest and most vulnerable persons in the centre and looking for their unique gifts. Adam was weaker and more vulnerable than anyone else at Daybreak, and Adam was given to me, the least capable of all, to care for . . . but not just to care for.

❧

Gradually, very gradually, things started to change,

and because I was more confident and relaxed, my mind and heart were opening for a real meeting with this man who had joined me on life's journey.

As I 'worked' with Adam I began to see myself right in the centre of Daybreak. How often Jean Vanier, the founder of L'Arche, had told me, 'L'Arche is not built around the word but around the body. We are so privileged to be entrusted with the body of another.' All my life had been shaped by words, ideas, books, and encyclopedias. But now my priorities were shifting. What was becoming important for me was Adam and our privileged time together when he offered me his body in total vulnerability, when he gave me himself, to be undressed, bathed, dressed, fed, and walked from place to place. Being close to Adam's body brought me close to Adam. I was slowly getting to know him.

I must confess that there were moments when I was impatient and preoccupied by what I was going to do when I had finished Adam's 'routine'. Then, without being conscious of his person, I started to rush him. Consciously, but mostly unconsciously, I hurriedly pushed his arms through his sleeves or his legs through his trousers. I wanted to be sure I was finished by 9 a.m. so I could go to my other work. Right here I learned that Adam could communicate! He let me know that I wasn't being really present to him and was more concerned about my schedule than about his. A few times when I was so pushy he responded by having a grand mal seizure, and I realised that it was his way of saying, 'Slow down, Henri! Slow down.' Well, it certainly slowed me down! A seizure so completely exhausted him that I had to stop everything I was doing and let him rest. Sometimes if it was a bad one, I brought him back to his bed and covered him with many blankets to keep him from shivering violently. Adam was communicating with me, and he was consistent in reminding me that he wanted and needed me to be with him unhurriedly and gently. He was clearly asking me if I was willing to follow his rhythm and adapt my ways to his needs. I found myself beginning to understand a new language, Adam's language.

I began to talk to Adam. I wasn't sure what he heard or understood, but I had a desire to let him know what I felt and what I thought about him, about me, about us. It didn't seem to matter to me any more that he could not respond in words. We were together, growing in friendship, and I was glad to be there. Before long Adam became my much trusted listener. I told him about the weather, about the day ahead of us, about his day and my work, about which of his clothes I liked most, about the kind of cereal I was going to give him, and about the people who were going to be with him during the day. Eventually I found myself confiding my secrets to him, telling him about my moods, my frustrations, my easy and hard relationships, and my prayer life. What was so amazing about all this was the very gradual realisation that Adam was really there for me, listening with his whole being and offering me a safe space to be. I wasn't expecting that, and though I do not express it well, it really happened.

As the weeks and months went by I grew attached to my one or two hours a day with Adam. They became my quiet hours, the most reflective and intimate time of the day. Indeed they became like a long prayer time. Adam kept 'telling' me in such a quiet way, 'Just be with me and trust that this is where you have to be . . . nowhere else.' Sometimes, while working in my office or talking to people, Adam came to my mind. I thought of him as a silent, peaceful presence in the centre of my life. Sometimes when I was anxious, irritated, or frustrated about something that wasn't happening well enough or fast enough, Adam came to mind and seemed to call me back to the stillness at the eye of the cyclone. The tables were turning, Adam was becoming *my* teacher, taking *me* by the hand, walking with me in my confusion through the wilderness of *my* life.

And there was more. My daily time with him had created a bond between us that was much deeper than I had originally realised. Adam was the one who was helping me to become rooted not just in Daybreak but in my own self. My closeness to him and to his body was bringing me closer to myself and to my own body. It was as if Adam kept pulling me back to earth, to the ground of being, to the source of life. My many words, spoken or written, always tempted me to go up into lofty ideas and perspectives without keeping in touch with the dailyness and beauty of ordinary life. Adam didn't allow this. It was as if he said to me, 'Not only do you *have* a body like I do, Henri, but you *are* your body. Don't let your words become separated from your flesh. Your words must become and remain flesh.' Adam was relating to me, was becoming central in my life. I started to experience a true relationship with and love for Adam.

Adam now was no longer a stranger to me. He was becoming a friend and a trustworthy companion, explaining to me by his very presence what I should have known all along: that what I most desire in life – love, friendship, community, and a deep sense of belonging – I was finding with him. His very gentle being was communicating with me in our moments together, and he began to educate me about love in a profoundly deep way. I am convinced that somewhere deep down Adam 'knew' that he was loved. He knew it in his very soul. Adam was not able to reflect on love, on the heart as the centre of our being, the core of our humanity where we give and receive love. He could not talk with me about the movements of his heart or my heart or the heart of God. He could explain nothing to me in words. But his heart was there, totally alive, full of love which he could both give and receive. Adam's heart made him fully alive.

As I grew closer to Adam, I came to experience his most beautiful heart as the gateway to his real self, to his person, his soul, and his spirit. His heart, so transparent, reflected for me not only his person but also the heart of the universe and, indeed, the heart of God. After my many years of studying, reflecting, and teaching theology, Adam came into my life, and by his life and his heart he announced to me and summarised all I had ever learned.

I always believed that the Word of God became flesh. I have preached that the divine became manifest in the human so that all things human could become manifestations of the divine. Adam came with others to worship and to hear me preach. He sat in front of me in his chair, and I 'saw' the divine significance made visible in him. Adam, I believe, had a heart where the Word of God was dwelling in intimate silence. Adam, during our time together, led me to that intimate indwelling where the deepest significance of his and my humanity was unfolding.

Adam's humanity was not diminished by his disabilities. Adam's humanity was a full humanity, in which the fullness of love became visible for me, and for others who grew to know him. Yes, I began to love Adam with a love that transcended most of the feelings, emotions, and passions that I had associated with love among people. Adam couldn't say, 'I love you', he couldn't embrace me spontaneously or express gratitude in words. Still I dare to say we loved each other with a love that was as enfleshed as any love, and was at the same time truly spiritual. We were friends, brothers, bonded in our hearts. Adam's love was pure and true. It was the same as the love that was mysteriously visible in Jesus, which healed everyone who touched him.

When I go to L'Arche meetings and retreats we are often asked to reflect on the questions: 'Who is the person in your home who showed you that people with disabilities have as much to give as to receive? Who rooted you in your community? Who inspired you to commit yourself to a life with women and men with disabilities? Who invited you to say yes to a life that from the outside looks so uninteresting and so marginal?' I always answer, 'Adam'. Adam was so completely dependent on us that he catapulted me to the essential, to the source. What is community? What is care? What is love? What is life? And who am I, who are we, who is God? Adam was so fully alive to me, and he shed light on all these questions. This experience cannot be understood by a logical explanation, but rather in and through the spiritual bonding of two very different people who discovered each other as completely equal in the heart of God. From my heart I could offer him some care that he really needed, and from his heart he blessed me with a pure and lasting gift of himself.

❦

How did I come to recognise all that was happening to me?

One day a few months after I had arrived at Daybreak a minister friend who had taught pastoral theology to many students for many years came to visit me. He arrived after I had completely shifted and forgotten my initial, narrow vision of Adam. Now I no longer thought of him as a stranger or even disabled. We were living together, and life for me with Adam and the others in the home was very 'normal'. I felt so privileged to be caring for Adam, and I was eager to introduce him to my guest.

When my friend came into the New House and saw me with Adam, he looked at me and asked, 'Henri, is this where you are spending your time?' I saw that he was not only disturbed but even angry. 'Did you leave the university, where you were such an inspiration to so many people, to give your time and energy to Adam? You aren't even trained for this! Why do you not leave this work to those who are trained for it? Surely you have better things to do with your time.'

I was shocked. My mind was racing, and I thought but did not say, 'Are you telling me that I am wasting my time with Adam? You, an experienced minister and a pastoral guide! Don't you see that Adam is my friend, my teacher, my spiritual director, my counsellor, my minister?' I quickly realised that he was not seeing the same Adam I was seeing. What my friend was saying made sense to him because he didn't really 'see' Adam, and he certainly wasn't prepared to get to know him.

My friend had a lot more questions about Adam and the people who lived with me in my home: 'Why spend so much time and money on people with severe disabilities while so many capable people can hardly survive?' And, 'Why should such people be allowed to take time and energy which should be given to solving the real problems humanity is facing?'

I didn't answer my friend's questions. I didn't argue or discuss his 'issues'. I felt deeply that I had nothing very intelligent to say that would change my friend's mind. My daily two hours with Adam were transforming me. In being present to him I was hearing an inner voice of love beyond all the activities of care. Those two hours were pure gift, a time of contemplation, during which we, together, were touching something of God. With Adam I knew a sacred presence and I 'saw' the face of God.

For many years I had reserved the word 'Incarnation' for the historic event of God's coming to us in Jesus. Being so close with Adam I realised that the 'Christ event' is much more than something that took place long ago. It occurs every time spirit greets spirit in the body. It is a sacred event happening in the present because it is God's event among people. That is what the sacramental life is all about. It is God's ongoing incarnation whenever people meet each other 'in God's name'. My relationship with Adam was giving me new eyes to see and new ears to hear. I was being changed much more than I ever anticipated.

I was only one in the long row of people who spent their time and energy with Adam. Except for his eight hours of sleep Adam was never alone. From nine in the morning until four in the afternoon at his day programme he was surrounded by men and women who walked with him, went swimming with him, did exercises with him, gave him massages, helped him with his lunch, and regularly changed his clothes. During all these hours people spoke with him, laughed with him, listened to music with him, and created a place where he felt safe and at home. When at four o'clock he returned home to the New House he could sit for a few hours in his reclining chair to doze and rest. Then it was dinnertime, the time Adam could show the little independence he had by hand-ling his own spoon and cup and surprising his guests with his solid appetite. After dinner there was prayer with songs. People held his hands or put their arms on his shoulders. Michael, Adam's brother, was a faithful visitor, who, like me, enjoyed sitting beside Adam, sometimes talking, but content and happy with long moments of silence in his presence. And Jeanne and Rex loved to take him home for weekends and holi-days and to visit often, walk with him, sit with him in the living room or in his bedroom, and whisper loving words into his ear. Each one had a relationship with Adam. Each one received gifts of peace, presence, safety, and love.

Could Adam pray? Did he know who God is and what the Name of Jesus means? Did he understand the mystery of God among us? For a long time I thought about these questions. For a long time I was curious about how much of what I knew, Adam could know, and how much of what I understood, Adam could understand. But now I see that these were questions from 'below', questions that reflected more my anxiety and uncertainty than God's love. God's questions, the questions from 'above', were, 'Can you let Adam lead you into prayer? Can you believe that I am in deep communion with Adam and that his life is a prayer? Can you let Adam be a living prayer at your table? Can you see my face in the face of Adam?'

And while I, the so-called 'normal' person, kept wondering how much Adam was like me, he had no need to make any comparisons. He simply lived and by his life invited me to receive his unique gift, wrapped in weakness but given for my transformation. While I tended to worry about what I did and how much I could produce, Adam was announcing to me that 'being is more important than doing'. While I was preoccupied with the way I was talked about or written about, Adam was quietly telling me that 'God's love is more important than the praise of people.' While I was concerned about my individual accomplishments, Adam was reminding me that 'doing things together is more important than doing things alone.' Adam couldn't produce anything, had no fame to be proud of, couldn't brag of any award or trophy. But by his very life, he was the most radical witness to the truth of our lives that I have ever encountered.

❦

It took me a long time to see this complete reversal of values, but once I experienced it, it was as if I was walking into completely new spiritual territory. I now understood more clearly what Jesus meant when he said, 'Blessed are your eyes because they see, your ears because they hear! In truth I tell you, many prophets and upright people longed to see what you see, and never saw it; to hear what you hear, and never heard it' (Matt. 13:16, 17). The great paradoxes of the Gospel – that the last will be the first, that those who lose their lives will gain them, that the poor are blessed, and that the gentle will inherit the Kingdom – all became incarnate for me in Adam.

There is nothing sweet or pious about this. Many men and women assisted Adam during the 11 years that he lived at Daybreak, and they all can tell stories about the gift of caring for him. When Adam came to the New House he was 22 years old. He certainly was not a thin man, not easy to hold and walk behind, and the many activities necessary to keep him in good physical shape were complex and tiring. Over the years quite a few people in the Daybreak community had learned his 'routine' so that they could be called upon when nobody in the house was free to help Adam. Adam's housemates, Rosie, Michael, John, and Roy, also needed a lot of attention. Rosie, who came to the New House at the same time as Adam, is no less disabled. Michael, who has not only a mental handicap but also severe cerebral palsy, needs assistance in every move he makes. John, who with Down's syndrome can go his own way, still requires much emotional support and attention. And Roy, who at the age of 80 is the oldest member of the community, needs constant emotional and physical support. The New House, with five or six assistants and five core members, is a very busy place, and the many assistants who have lived and worked there didn't always think about Adam in the way I have described him. At the same time, what prevented them from perceiving themselves as housecleaners, cooks, nappy changers, and dishwashers was the experience that Adam, Rosie, Michael, John, and Roy, who were entrusted to them, had as much to give them as to receive from them. Many of them touched into the mystery of their own lives and experienced a renewal of their inner selves, mainly because they were able to receive some spiritual gift from the people they were caring for.

Speaking about 'Adam's gift' is not romanticising

an otherwise quite demanding and unrewarding life situation. Adam's gift was a reality of everyday living. When, on Monday mornings, Jane, D.J., and the other assistants gathered to discuss the week that had passed and the week to come, the main questions always were, 'What was difficult for you this week?' and, 'What was the gift you gave and the gift you received?' Amid all the planning of meals, clean ups, visits to the doctor, shopping, repairs, and countless other things to do, that question of the gifts of Adam, Roy, Michael, Rosie, and John always remained central. Everyone knew that they would not remain good L'Arche assistants for long if they weren't richly rewarded – by the spiritual gifts of people like Rosie and John. They were discovering that true care is mutual care. If their only reward had been the small salary, their care would soon have become little more than human maintenance. Not only would they have become bored, exhausted, and deeply frustrated, but Adam and the others would not have been able to give their gifts, accomplish their mission, or reach the fulfilment of their human potential.

❦

Adam and the other core members were announcing Good News. Adam kept reminding us that the beauty of caregiving was not just in giving but also in receiving from him. He was the one who opened me to the realisation that the greatest gift I could offer to him was my open hand and open heart to receive from him his precious gift of peace. In this exchange I was enriched and so was he. I was able to reveal to him that he had a gift to offer, and his true gift became a gift when I welcomed it. He gave his gift freely to everyone he met, and so many people received it and were enriched by it. Caring, he kept 'telling' us, is as much receiving as giving, as much giving thanks as asking for it, as much affirming him in his ability to give as looking for self-affirmation. Caring for Adam was allowing Adam to care for us as we cared for him. Only then did Adam and his assistants grow in mutuality and fruitfulness. Only then was our care for Adam not burdensome, but privileged because Adam's care for us bore fruit in our lives.

And, in this milieu of mutual caring, Adam was able to live a public life beyond the confines of Daybreak. Sometimes true 'miracles' happened. During and after my time in the New House I saw remarkable changes in people, which happened as a direct consequence of their contact with Adam.

My friend Murray, a New York businessman, husband of Peggy, and father of nine children, called me at Daybreak. He had heard about me through friends and had read several of my books. When he realised that I was leaving the university to live with people with mental disabilities he was quite shocked. He wanted to do anything in his power to make sure

I didn't stop writing. Being a man deeply involved in the financial world and having many friends there, he proposed creating a circle of people who would offer me a yearly gift that would enable me to keep writing even as I held the low-paying role of pastor for handicapped people.

Often he said, 'Henri, you don't know anything about money; you are a writer. Let me help you with money, and you can help us with your writings.' Murray was a deeply religious man who was quite concerned that his children would become so preoccupied with making money and pursuing successful careers that they would lose contact with their spiritual heritage. 'You have to keep my kids close to God,' he would say.

I first met Murray at the New York Athletic Club. Soon after that he and Peggy welcomed me in their summer house in Ireland, and a little later I came to know most of the family in their home in Peapack, New Jersey. I will never forget sitting at the dinner table with at least 12 people, Murray at one end and I at the other. After grace Murray said, 'Now, Henri, talk to my kids' – they were all in their twenties and thirties! – 'and make them go to church again.' The 'children', all very articulate, well-educated men and women, showed much sympathy for their father's well-intentioned attempt, but they were not afraid to let him and me know how little, if anything, they expected from going to church. A fierce but loving debate followed, showing that there was a lot more religion around the table than Murray had assumed.

I developed a real friendship with Murray's family. Then one day I said, 'Murray, it is time for you to visit me at Daybreak. Please come and stay with me for a few days.' Murray hesitated. He felt that his task was to keep me writing, not to get involved in my life with disabled people. In fact he wondered if I wasn't wasting my time with these 'poor people'. But after some more persuasion, he accepted. When I told him that I wanted him to stay with me in the New House and that our little basement guest room was ready for him, he looked more than puzzled. 'I think I might be better off in a hotel,' he suggested. But I insisted: 'No, no, you will love it just being with us, and you will have a chance to meet Adam.'

Meeting Adam wasn't why Murray thought he had come to see me. But reluctantly he went along with my proposal. We enjoyed a pleasant, noisy dinner at the New House, where Murray was attentive, but said little. Murray followed me around for a couple of days, meeting people, visiting some of the other homes, and 'observing' my relationship with Adam. To my great surprise, Murray was quite comfortable in the home. He didn't say much but he was just there.

One morning at the breakfast table Murray and I sat quietly, close to Adam. Murray watched every one of his moves, and he watched me as I supported him to bring his spoon to his mouth and to hold his orange juice glass. Suddenly, there was a phone call asking me to go to my office. I quickly told Adam that I was sorry I had to leave in a hurry but that he would be in good hands. Then I said to Murray, 'I have to leave for a while. Why don't you help Adam finish his breakfast and afterwards the assistants will help Adam get off to work.' Murray said, 'Fine', although I didn't realise how anxious he felt.

Murray told me later that during the next 30 minutes as he sat with Adam he began to recognise him not as a disabled man completely different from himself, but as a beautiful human being who shared with him many vulnerabilities. Although Murray was a very successful businessman, he had his own struggles, his own fears, his own experiences of failure, his own disabilities. Sitting beside Adam, helping him with his breakfast, was for Murray a moment of grace as he realised that he and Adam were brothers. Distance fell away, and a deep compassion emerged in Murray's heart, a connectedness with Adam, who drew him close and gave him light. The day that followed was a truly new day for Murray. He told me later how he went about with a new feeling of being accepted, loved, and appreciated – not just by Adam but by all the people in the New House.

Murray's visit to Daybreak bore many fruits in his life, opening him more to accept his own brokenness and failure and to be less defensive among his family and friends. It certainly deepened our friendship. From then on Murray spoke about Adam with great love, and whenever he called he always asked, 'And how is Adam?'

Four years after his trip to Toronto, Murray had a sudden and fatal heart attack. His death was a very painful loss for Peggy, his children, his family and friends, and me. As I spoke at his memorial service, I remembered that Adam had played an important role in helping Murray to face with less fear his own vulnerabilities, thus preparing him for his final passage to God.

❦

Murray's story doesn't stand alone. Countless people who came to the New House for a week, a day, or only a few hours were deeply affected by Adam's beautiful, silent presence. Some told me that when they returned home they kept thinking of him and talking about him with their friends. Their encounters with Adam often became experiences of inner renewal because he offered them an opportunity and a context to think differently about their lives, their goals, their aspirations. Adam offered those he met a presence and a safe space to recognise and accept their own, often invisible, disabilities. He radiated peace from his centre, which supported people as they lived through difficult times or had important choices to make. Not everyone who met him had the same experience with

Adam. For some it was an experience of peace, and for others self-confrontation; for some it was a rediscovery of their hearts, and for others it meant nothing.

Adam's ministry was unique in that he seemed unaware of all that was happening around and through him because he didn't know about care, ministry, healing, or service. He seemed to be without concepts, plans, intentions, or aspirations. He was simply present, offering himself in peace and completely self-emptied so that the fruits of his ministry were pure and abundant. I can witness that the words said of Jesus could be said of Adam: 'Everyone who touched him was healed' (Mark 6:56).

Adam was a true teacher and a true healer. Most of his healing was inner healing that announced peace, courage, joy, and freedom to those who often were hardly able to acknowledge their wounds. Adam, by his eyes and by his presence, said to us, 'Don't be afraid. You don't have to run away from your pain. Look at me, be close to me, and you will discover that you are God's beloved child, just as I am.'

For that reason I do not think it is an exaggeration to say that Daybreak was the place of Adam's public ministry. It is my firm belief that Adam, like Jesus, was sent into the world to fulfil his unique mission. During his years at home with his family, he lived the mutuality of love, growing in stature while transforming his parents. It was the preparation. In

Daybreak his gifts, his teaching, and his healing had a deep impact on the many people who came to live with him as well as on those who came to visit or to live in other homes in the community.

❦

CHAPTER FOUR

Adam's Way

DURING THE ELEVEN YEARS that Adam lived in the New House many assistants came and went. Some were from Canada and the United States, others from Australia, Germany, Brazil, Poland, the Ukraine, and many other countries. They often came for one or two years to explore a new direction in life and have a 'different' experience away from home. A few found their permanent vocation in L'Arche, but most of them went on to become lawyers, social workers, therapists, nurses, or businessmen and women.

In addition, countless people came for visits. The New House, even though it is one of the busiest houses in Daybreak, is one of the most hospitable. 'Come for dinner tonight!' is a familiar invitation, and many people from other Daybreak houses or from far-away cities and countries join members for a meal and experience the pains and joys of this unique household. The table is often decorated with flowers and candles, and the food is prepared with great care, taking into account the various dietary requirements.

There is usually good conversation, and often prayers, songs, and music after the meal. Seldom are there fewer than 12 people around the table, and often there are many more.

During his time at the New House Adam must have met hundreds of people. Many newcomers experienced uneasiness, and even fear, when they first encountered the core members, who were so visibly different from them. But one hour around the dinner table was enough to take most of their nervousness away, and most of those who came to the New House will remember Adam as the quiet centre of the house. Somehow Adam impressed himself on their hearts and minds. Often they would write: 'Give my love to Adam.' 'Give him a kiss and hug for me.' 'Tell him that I am thinking of him and you all.'

The dinner table at the New House was where most of Adam's 'miracles' took place. He obviously did not *do* anything. He just was there. But his 'being there' touched people's hearts and souls in a profound way. There were no sudden cures, no immediate changes of heart, but there was a discovery that he, we, and the whole world had a new meaning, a new significance, a new purpose.

Some of Adam's miracles were so personal and took place so deep in the heart they cannot be shared in words. Some of them occurred months or years after the person had visited. And some required the person to make a radical turnaround. I still remember a woman visiting the New House, walking right up to Adam, and saying, 'Poor man, poor man, why did this happen to you? Let me pray over you so that our dear Lord may heal you.' She motioned the assistants to make a circle around Adam to pray. But one of them gently tapped her on the shoulder and said, 'Adam doesn't need any healing; he is fine. He is just happy that you came for dinner. Please join us at the table.' I do not know whether this visitor was ever ready to be touched by Adam, to see his wholeness and holiness in his brokenness, but she did come to realise that everyone in the house was very happy with Adam the way he was.

There is no doubt that Adam's 'way' of being and of living had a profound impact on the lives of those who encountered him, not least of all myself. Three stories come to mind, that concern Father Bruno, my friend Cathy, and myself.

❦

About a year after I had become the full-time minister of Daybreak and had moved into our little retreat house and chapel called the Dayspring, a middle-aged priest arrived for a sabbatical. Father Bruno had just finished his 18-year term as abbot of the Carnaldolese monastery in Big Sur, California, and he needed a time away from his community. He was a tall, thin man with a short beard, gentle eyes, and a peaceful disposition, very soft-spoken, but mostly silent and a little shy. A true monk. Why had he come to us? He had heard about Daybreak and thought it might be a good place for him to make the transition from carrying authority to being an ordinary monk again. He wanted to share in the life of handicapped people. During his three months with us he lived in the New House. Soon after he arrived I saw him often on the lane and on the public road pushing Adam in his wheelchair. Since he was not an ordinary assistant but a long-term guest, he had lots of extra time and had decided to spend much of it with Adam. The two of them seemed to enjoy just being in each other's company.

As I saw them together I thought, 'What better companion could Adam have than this quiet, peaceful monk! Isn't Adam's life similar to his? Peace is speaking to peace. Solitude is greeting solitude. Silence is dwelling with silence. What a grace!'

One day Bruno dropped by my room for a visit. I asked, 'How are you and Adam doing?' Bruno looked at me, full of wonder and delight. He said, 'Adam is truly a gift to me. He is teaching me how to be a better monk.' I answered, 'I think I know what you mean but please try to explain it to me.'

Bruno wasn't a great talker. He felt things deeply and preferred to remain silent about them. Nevertheless, he wanted to explain what he was experiencing with Adam. He said, 'For many, many years I have tried to live a spiritual life and have tried to help others live it as well. I always knew that I had to become empty for God, gradually letting go of thoughts, emotions, feelings, and passions that prevented the deep communion with God I desired. When I met Adam, I met a man who has been chosen by God to lead us deeper into that very communion. As I spend long hours with Adam, I find myself drawn into an ever deeper solitude. In Adam's heart, I have touched a fullness of divine love.'

I couldn't avoid thinking about Adam and how his truth and his life had been cause for Bruno's extraordinary spiritual experience. An abbot, a father of monks, had found a guide, a spiritual master, in the person of Adam.

❦

As the years passed, I came to think of Adam as someone who might be able to help people I couldn't help. More and more people were coming to Daybreak to make retreats, receive spiritual direction, or just find a little solitude and silence in their busy lives. Sometimes they came with very concrete struggles, hoping to meet someone who could offer perspective, relief, maybe some healing. Several people in the community tried to respond to the needs of our many visitors, and we were increasingly surprised to see how a few days of silence and good spiritual direction in the context of a community of love could help.

But sometimes we wondered if people weren't

expecting too much. It was in one of these situations that Adam helped us out. This is the story of Cathy.

One day a black stretch limousine with darkened windows turned in to the Daybreak property. Several people who saw the car were quite puzzled. Why would anyone who drives around in such a vehicle ever come to Daybreak?

When the limousine came to a stop in front of the Dayspring, a short, very thin woman emerged. 'I am Cathy,' she said. 'I have come from New York City and need some help with my problems.' Sister Sue Mosteller, the host of the Dayspring, and I led her into the house. 'How can we help you?' we asked.

'Well, to be frank with you,' she said, 'I am terribly depressed. I have been seeing a psychiatrist for many years now, and he hasn't been able to help me. On the contrary, it is getting worse and worse. So my brother, who knows about Daybreak, said to me, "Why don't you go there? Maybe those people can help you". So, here I am.' She must have been at least 70 years old. She had a lovely face, and there was a little sparkle in her eyes. She was meticulously dressed and seemed quite self-possessed. Why would she be depressed?

Sue said, 'Can you tell us a little bit more? Are there any events that trigger your depression?'

'Oh, yes,' Cathy replied. 'It might sound strange to you, but every time I look in the social section of the *New York Times* and read the names of all the people who have been invited by the President of the United States and the First Lady to the White House for lunch, I get depressed because I am not on the list!'

Sue and I looked at each other. This was new territory for us!

Cathy went on, 'I am always comparing myself to others, and as I get older I realise that more and more people forget me. And then when I see that people who have not even half the money I have or half the connections are more desirable than I am, I get very, very depressed.'

Then Cathy started to tell us about her life – her prestigious marriage, her children, her divorce, her second marriage, her busy social life, her relationship with the church, her charitable work, and her fame. She told all of this very directly, honestly, and not without a sense of humour. 'People always expect money from me,' she said. 'Whenever I lose something I promise St Anthony that I will give the church a thousand dollars when I find it. Nowadays, when I go to Mass the pastor asks me, "Cathy, did you lose something this week?" '

Gradually a most unusual but tragic picture emerged. Here was a woman who had everything a human being can dream of – money, fame, connections, and great power – wondering whether anyone really loved her. Rich but poor. Famous but self-doubting. Great but very small.

Sue said, 'Cathy, do you believe that you are a good person simply because you are Cathy?'

Tears came to her eyes. She said, 'I don't know. I don't even know who I am without all the stuff that surrounds me. I don't know what it would mean if people loved me simply as Cathy. Would they? I often wonder!'

Suddenly her depression made sense to me. Cathy was asking the same question we all are asking: If people knew us as we really are, without all the worldly decorations we have gathered, would they still love us? Or would they forget us as soon as we were no longer of use to them? This is the central question of identity: Are we good because of what we do or have, or because of who we are? Am I somebody because the world makes me into somebody, or am I somebody because I belonged to God long before I belonged to the world? So much had happened in Cathy's long life that she had lost contact with the original, uncomplicated, lovable person she was.

The more Sue and I talked to her, the more we realised that no argument would ever help her to love herself. In fact, we ourselves were not completely free from the entrapments Cathy spoke about. We too were impressed by her wealth and fame. Would she ever be able to accept from us her true spiritual self? It wouldn't take much for her to come to think of us as she thought of everyone else: potential users. As I became aware of how hard it would be for Cathy to be set free from her social prison, Adam came to my mind. He was perhaps the only one who would never use her in any way. He would not ask her for money, he was not looking for fame, and he did not need to impress anyone.

I said, 'Cathy, you are invited to the New House for dinner tonight. You will be with Adam and his housemates.' She was a little surprised. Why should she have a meal with handicapped people when she had come to get spiritual help? I could see the question in her eyes even though she said politely, 'I would love to go and see your poor people.' At the last minute I decided not to go with her. I wanted her to be the only guest.

When Cathy returned from dinner at 9 p.m., I was waiting for her, somewhat anxious about whether I had done the right thing. But when she walked into the living room she was relaxed and happy. 'Henri,' she said, 'that was so good. I felt very accepted, even cared for, and welcome. I think they really liked me. I must say that I was fearful when you first asked me to go, but I was quite happy to be there. Everyone was kind and friendly. And I connected with Adam, maybe because I sat beside him and was able to help him a little bit. What a beautiful man he is. Really, the whole evening was wonderful.'

I could hardly believe the change in her expression and in her eyes. Was this our depressed visitor? I noticed that she had a chocolate bar in her hand. 'Well, well,' I said. 'You won the candy bar from John!'

'Yes, John got up after dinner and gave a speech, of which I couldn't understand a word. Then he asked each of us to give him a number and to mention the colour of our clothes. We did. He looked at the notepad in his hand and declared that I had won the prize. He walked up to me and gave me the chocolate bar as well as a kiss. I could hardly believe it. But I felt so welcomed there and these people do not even know me!'

What a gift and what a mystery! One of the wealthiest people in our world, deeply grateful for a chocolate bar. Adam, John, Rosie, Roy, and Michael had been able to remind her of her truth as Cathy, a beautiful person.

After she returned to New York Cathy called and said, 'My husband is aware that something important happened to me at Daybreak. He wanted to know what we did when I was there. I told him about my dinner in the New House and about Adam and John and the chocolate bar. I do not feel that awful depression that I had before. Inside of me there is a new sense of God, and of God's love for me.'

In the years that followed Cathy and I spoke often by telephone, and twice I visited her. She kept assuring me, 'Something quite profound happened on my visit to Daybreak. I am no longer as depressed as I was before because I feel more connected with myself,' and I could see that she spoke the truth. She had many physical problems and suffered much pain, but her depression had lifted.

When Cathy died, eight years after her visit to Daybreak, her family asked me to lead her funeral service. I protested: 'Why me? She knew so many priests.' But they said, 'No, we want you to do it because she was always so grateful to you and the Daybreak community.' I accepted, and I told the many family members and friends who had come to her funeral that God blessed Cathy not only in her gifts but also in her poverty, because of her willingness to receive a gift of healing from Adam and a chocolate bar from John. I don't know if they could understand what I said, but I wanted to tell everyone that a very poor man had done something miraculous for a very poor woman.

❦

Finally there is the story of how Adam's authentic way of life pointed me, or rather drove me into the deeper realisation of my own. I lived in the New House for 14 months. I was happy to be there, and my relationship with Adam grew deeper and stronger as the days passed. But a very painful time was ahead of me. It was the last thing I expected to happen. After my many years of teaching, Daybreak had become my home, where I could live in community, spend time in prayer, and care for 'the poor'. I had always been looking for a place where I could feel safe. Although the universities where I taught had given me a unique opportunity to develop my thinking about the spiritual life and to share my ideas with hundreds of students, they had not offered me a home. Daybreak did. I felt loved, appreciated, and cared for, and I never questioned that I had made the right move by joining L'Arche.

Still, something else was going on. Living close to Adam and the others brought me closer to my own vulnerabilities. While at first it seemed quite obvious who was handicapped and who was not, living together day in and day out made the boundaries less clear. Yes, Adam, Rosie, and Michael couldn't speak, but I spoke too much. Yes, Adam and Michael couldn't walk, but I was running around as if life was one emergency after the other. Yes, John and Roy needed help in their daily tasks, but I, too, was constantly saying, 'Help me, help me.' And when I had the courage to look deeper, to face my emotional neediness, my inability to pray, my impatience and restlessness, my many anxieties and fears, the word 'handicap' started to have a whole new meaning. The fact that my handicaps were less visible than those of Adam and his housemates didn't make them less real.

I began to realise that the gentle safety of the New House was weakening many of the defences I had created around my inner handicaps. In this loving, caring milieu, without competition, one-upmanship, and great pressure to distinguish myself, I experienced what I had not been able to see or experience before. I was faced with a very insecure, needy, and fragile person: myself. Looking out from this vantage point I saw Adam as the strong one. He was always there, quiet, peaceful, and inwardly steady. Adam, Rosie, Michael, John, and Roy – they all showed themselves to me as the solid core of our community.

Towards the end of 1987 I realised that I was heading for a crisis. I wasn't sleeping well and I was preoccupied by a friendship that had seemed life-giving but had gradually become suffocating for me. It was as if the planks that had covered my emotional abyss had been taken away and I was looking into a canyon full of wild animals waiting to devour me. I found myself overwhelmed by intense feelings of abandonment, rejection, neediness, dependence, despair. Here I was in the most peaceful house, with the most peaceful people, but raging inside myself.

I spoke to a few members of my community, at first obliquely but then quite openly and directly. I soon found myself speaking to a psychiatrist. Everyone said the same thing: 'It is time for you to face your demons. It is time to bind your own wounds, to let others care for you.'

It was a very humbling proposal. I had to leave the New House and the community for a place where I could live through my anguish in the hope of finding new strength and new peace. What did it all mean? I didn't know. I had come to live in community and to care for Adam. Now I had to leave Adam to others and fully acknowledge my own disabilities.

I was going through the deep human struggle to believe in my belovedness even when I had nothing to be proud of. Yes, I had left the university with its prestige, but this life gave me satisfaction and even brought me admiration. Yes, I was considered a good, even a noble person because I was helping the poor! But now that the last crutch had been taken away, I was challenged to believe that even when I had nothing to show for myself, I was still God's beloved son.

As I lived through this emotional ordeal I realised that I was becoming like Adam. He had nothing to be proud of. Neither had I. He was completely empty. So was I. He needed full-time attention. So did I. I found myself resisting this 'becoming like Adam'. I did not want to be dependent and weak. I did not want to be so needy. Somewhere though I recognised that Adam's way, the way of radical vulnerability, was also the way of Jesus.

During the months that I spent away from Daybreak I was able – with much guidance – to hear a soft and gentle inner voice saying, 'You are my beloved child, on you my favour rests.' For a long time I distrusted that voice. I kept saying to myself, 'It is a lie. I know the truth. There is nothing in me worth loving.' But my guides were there, encouraging me to listen to that voice and let it become stronger. When I finally was able to put my trust in that voice I was ready to go home to Daybreak and continue my life there.

The community did not ask me to return to the New House or to continue working with Adam. That intimate time that I had spent helping Adam had come to an end. Other people had taken my place. I was invited to widen my ministry as Daybreak's pastor.

In retrospect, I see that Adam's and my relationship changed after my return. For 14 months he had been my teacher and guide. He had rooted me in the Daybreak community, opened my heart to the gift of vulnerability, and led me to confront my own abyss. Now, having discovered the inner voice of love and having put my trust in it, I no longer needed to be with him so constantly. Now we could be friends, members of the same community, two men journeying together to God. Our poverties had touched each other and our relationship was sound.

I remained a special friend of the New House. Whenever possible I came for a meal and always was given a seat beside Adam. When Adam celebrated his birthday his assistants always invited me to the party.

Bruno, Cathy and I were only three of many recipients of Adam's truth and life. Just as Jesus had said to Philip, 'Whoever has seen me, has seen the Father,' so we were privileged to catch a glimpse of God's presence in Adam (John 14:9). I believe that God sent Adam as God sent Jesus, to be an instrument of grace, a source of healing, a cause of new joy. He was so whole, so peaceful, silent, breathing heavily, fidgeting with his fingers, and never aware of how special he was.

In our society plagued by fear, anxiety, loneliness, depression, and a sense of being lost, we keep looking for guides. We so much hope that someone – a guru, spiritual director, or soul friend – can help us make sense out of our confusion and can show us a way to inner wholeness, freedom, and peace. We look mostly for men and women with a reputation, with wisdom, psychological insight, spiritual sensitivity, and solid life experience. Perhaps the problem is that we expect too much, and they want to give too much. Then we become dependent and they become controlling.

Adam was the least controlling and the most dependent guide I ever encountered. Maybe that's why I was able to put so much confidence in his way. I believe he worked miracles like the miracles of Jesus precisely because he never claimed any of them for himself. He didn't ask for money, fame, or even thanks. In his total powerlessness Adam was a pure instrument of God's healing power for Bruno, for Cathy, and, most of all, for me.

CHAPTER FIVE

❧

Adam's Passion

THE WORD 'passion' is derived from the Latin verb *patior*, which means 'to undergo'. It is related to the word 'passive'.

Jesus' passion came after much action. For three years he went from village to village, town to town, preaching, teaching, responding to people's questions, healing the sick, confronting the hypocrites, consoling the sorrowing, calling the dead back to life. Wherever he went there were large crowds of people admiring him, listening to him, asking him for help. During these intense, nearly hectic years Jesus was in control of the situation. He came and went as he felt it was right for him to do. His disciples accepted his leadership and followed him wherever he went.

But at Gethsemane – the Garden of Olives – all this action came to a sudden end. There Jesus was handed over by one of his own disciples to undergo suffering. That's where his passion began. From that moment on he could no longer *do* anything; everything was done to him. He was arrested, put in prison, led before Herod and Pilate, flagellated, crowned with thorns, given a cross to carry, stripped of his clothes, nailed on the cross, and ridiculed until he died. He could no longer act. He was only acted upon. It was pure passion.

The great mystery of Jesus' life is that he fulfilled his mission not in action but in passion, not by what he did but by what was done to him, not by his own decision but by other people's decisions concerning him. It was when he was dying on the cross that he cried out, 'It is fulfilled.'

Adam's whole life was passion, a life of suffering in which he underwent everything that was done for him, to him, with him, and around him. His was primarily the suffering of complete dependence on other people's actions and decisions. He could only take a few initiatives – like jumping on his bed, or pushing the vacuum cleaner down the stairs, or lifting his spoon or cup – but he could never determine where to go, with whom to be, or what to do. Adam lived every moment of his life waiting for others to act on his behalf.

He had a few years when his health was stable, but the main question always was: How can we control his epileptic seizures? He suffered seizures every day, seizures that sometimes so exhausted him that he had to recuperate in bed. His anti-epileptic medication helped to control the seizures but had side-effects and other disadvantages. It took away his energy, made him constipated, drowsy, and always, over time, filled his system with toxins. Many visits to the hospital were necessary to find a balance in his medications. When he got toxic, Adam had to spend time in the hospital under close observation to allow his doctor to determine the right amount and strength of the anti-epileptic drugs. And what no one knew until the end of his life was that the consistency of the drug programme was weakening his heart.

ಌ

We do not know about many of his physical or any of his emotional pains or struggles. Perhaps one of his biggest sufferings was that Adam couldn't tell anyone what was bothering him. When Rex or Jeanne noticed, for example, that his teeth had disappeared into his gums, they could act quickly for Adam, but it was more difficult to know the problem when he had the hearing aids or was being overdosed. It meant that so much guessing was necessary to find the causes for his obvious discomfort.

His health was generally fragile, up and down. Adam's breathing was always laboured, heavy and irregular. Just breathing took a lot out of him, and this problem seemed to become worse with age. Whenever he had a cold or flu, he needed a long recuperation time to regain strength and energy.

In the autumn of 1994 Adam became very ill. Nobody knew exactly what the matter was, but he was rushed to the emergency section of York-Central Hospital in Richmond Hill. When I arrived a little later, Rex and Jeanne were already there, and Ann Pavilonis, the head of the New House, was talking to the nurses and doctors. 'He has double pneumonia,' Ann told me when she returned. 'The doctors aren't sure if they can pull him through.' We gathered around Adam's bed. He was hooked up on several monitors, and he seemed unconscious.

Ann said, 'The doctor is asking Rex and Jeanne whether to put Adam on a respirator when the situation gets critical.' A little later we all talked. Rex and Jeanne were very clear: 'We want Adam to live as long as possible and to suffer as little as possible.' They wanted a respirator to be used only as a temporary measure. They couldn't imagine Adam living the rest of his life on such a mechanism. 'He has suffered enough,' Jeanne said.

But Adam wasn't ready to die. The next morning he was doing a lot better, and a week later he was back home.

For me it was a first realisation of how fragile Adam's health was. I had never seriously thought about losing him. He was only 33 years old, and although he needed much medical attention, he seemed strong enough to live a long life. But Adam remained quite weak and never fully recovered from this bout of double pneumonia. We realised that he had been very close to death and that we had to start thinking of the possibility that his life would be short. It was hard for us to hold on to this possibility so we sometimes forgot about it – with the exception of Ann, the nurse responsible for the New House. Adam was the centre of that house and his continuing weakness was Ann's great concern. Doctors told her that there wasn't anything they could do to help Adam get stronger, but they didn't say much about his heart. Life went on, but for many months Adam could not go to his day programme and spent most of his days either in bed or in his chair in the dining room, the soul of the home. Rex and Jeanne, his faithful and loving parents, came more often as their son entered into the final stages of his passion.

The assistants in his home and his day programme were wonderful. They may have found it difficult to set up a rota so that someone was always there with Adam, but they did not complain that they lost some of their 'free time'. Each one of them spent long hours being with Adam, feeding him when he was too weak to do it himself, changing him, and finding ways to give him the special foods which he so enjoyed. Adam's profound and continuing weakness sometimes frightened them too, especially because they were responsible for his direct care. These were all young people, many of whom had never been close to those who were chronically ill or dying. They asked, 'What if he has a seizure and doesn't wake up? What if he should die when I am the only one in the house? What if he collapses when I'm giving him a bath? What if something happens in the night?' These were their real concerns, seemingly having more to do with themselves than with Adam. But they needed confidence to be able to be there for him. The months went on with only slight improvement, but because there were no emergencies we all settled in, and some of us became accustomed to Adam's precarious health.

Jeanne, Rex, Michael, and Adam always spent Christmas together as a family. They had established traditions over the years which were important for them. On Christmas Eve they decorated the tree, drank hot apple cider, and Michael examined the gifts that were beautifully wrapped under the tree. Two events were important on Christmas Day: the gifts and the dinner.

That year Adam was too weak to go home for Christmas. After dinner on Christmas Day Michael and his parents came to the New House to visit Adam. They spent the day after Christmas together in the New House. It was not easy for Adam or for his parents, because Adam was visibly distressed, breathing heavily and very tired, and because Christmas was not the same without him at home.

A year later, the Christmas of 1995, Adam was just home from the hospital after another bout of pneumonia and once again was too weak to go home. Jeanne and Rex decided to come to the New House

for Christmas Day and to spend it there together with
Michael and Adam. Jeanne brought everything but
the turkey, and John David, Adam's friend and
assistant, cooked a breast of turkey for the Arnetts.
Everyone else left so that the family could have dinner
together. About 35 other members of the community
were having dinner next door in the large meeting
hall of Daybreak. Jeanne recalls that this Christmas
was better than the last one, but that Adam was so
weak she wanted to leave him in his chair and feed
him. Rex thought he might like to come to the table.
When dinner was ready, his dad brought Adam to the
table and the family enjoyed the meal together. Adam
was able to feed himself, and he thoroughly enjoyed
his meal – just like old times!

❦

All the action around Adam did nothing to decrease
his passion. He lived in total and utter dependency.
He seemed deeply resigned to it, totally given into
the hands of others, radiating light and peace in his
utter weakness. When I think of it today I realise how
none of us wanted to face the truth that he was
approaching the end of his passion.

Adam's passion for me was a profound prophetic
witness. His life and especially his passion radically
criticised those of us who give ourselves to the norms
of a society driven by individualism, materialism, and
sensationalism. Adam's total dependence made it pos-

sible for him to live fully only if we lived in a loving community around him. His great teaching to us was, 'I can live only if you surround me with love and if you love one another. Otherwise, my life is useless and I am a burden.' Adam clearly challenged us to trust that compassion, not competition, is the way to fulfil our human vocation. This challenge forced us to re-examine all the basic assumptions of our individual and action-oriented lives.

The truth is that a very large, if not the largest part of our lives is passion. Although we all want to act on our own, be independent and self-sufficient, we are for long periods of time dependent on other people's decisions. Not only when we are young and inexperienced or when we are old and needy but also when we are strong and self-reliant. Substantial parts of our success, wealth, health, and relationships are influenced by events and circumstances over which we have little or no control. We like to keep up the illusion of action as long as we can, but the fact is that passion is what finally determines the course of our life. We need people, loving and caring people, to sustain us during the times of our passion and thus support us to accomplish our mission. That, to me, is the final significance of Adam's passion: a radical call to accept the truth of our lives and to choose to give our love when we are strong and to receive the love of others when we are weak, always with tranquillity and generosity.

CHAPTER SIX

❦

Adam's Death

I N SEPTEMBER 1995, months after Adam's first bout
of pneumonia, I left Daybreak on a sabbatical year.
The whole previous year had been full of celebrations
connected with the twenty-fifth anniversary of the
community. I realised I needed a break, a time for
inner renewal and writing.

But it was not easy for me to leave the Daybreak
community. I had become very connected with the
daily life of the core members and their assistants. It
was now nine years since I had first arrived at the
New House and been introduced to Adam. Still, it
was time to take a few steps back from it all, to gather
up these years of pastoral work, and to start thinking
about the last phase of my life.

Around Christmastime, while I was spending a few
weeks with my 93-year-old father in Europe, I heard
from Ann Pavilonis that Adam was not doing well,
and that he had been unable to go home for
Christmas or to attend the celebrations in the community. That he and his family had spent Christmas

Day together in the New House and that Adam was too weak to go to his day programme. Ann is a wonderful and competent nurse and she told me, 'The doctors have found that he has an enlarged heart and they do not think he will live long. He is so weak. We are all quite afraid of the days ahead and of losing him. . . . Just pray that we will live it well.'

The weeks that followed were extremely hard for Adam, for his parents, and for each of the people in the New House. Adam went back and forth to the hospital quite a few times, and twice he was hospitalised for a full week. I was told that Rosie and Michael, his housemates who don't speak, really lived this time in solidarity and compassion with Adam. They had been together for 10 years, and they were deeply bonded to one another. Roy and John, who seem to be fearful around death, were unwilling to talk about Adam, but they also knew that his condition was worsening and they followed all the conversations about him and all the movement around him with great attention. The assistants who were bonded with Adam wanted to care for him at home, but his situation was so precarious that they realised it was not going to be good for him or for them.

❦

In early February Adam was admitted to the hospital in a critical condition. Doctors told Jeanne, Rex, and Ann that his heart was simply worn out, and the muscles were in shreds. There was nothing, short of a heart transplant, that would save him. This was surprising and devastating news for Adam's parents. Because doctors had not mentioned that Adam had a bad heart, they were not conscious that his condition was so serious. They were not prepared for the realisation that he would die so soon. Rex seriously considered asking for a transplant, but knew that Adam's quality of life would not be improved. As he let go of that last hope, he had to face the stark reality in front of him. He and Jeanne spent most of their time in the hospital, encouraging Adam as he breathed, then paused for long moments, then breathed again. They kept calling him to live and telling him that he could do it. Adam was listening and doing his best to respond to their deep and loving invitation to live. Assistants took turns to be there through the nights so that Adam was never left alone.

In the early morning of Monday, 12 February, Ann saw that the monitors to which Adam was connected were showing flat lines. When the doctor arrived there was no heartbeat, so he turned the monitor off, saying that Adam had suffered heart failure and was dead. The nurse, before leaving, lowered the bed so that Ann could be alone with Adam's body. 'As soon as they left,' Ann recalls, 'I rolled the bed back up and began to talk to Adam. I cannot tell you all I said because my language was very strong, but I basically, and in no uncertain terms, told him that his parents weren't here yet and he simply could not die until they came! I knew they were on the way. I rubbed his chest and I talked loudly, calling him to listen to me! After a few minutes, Adam took a deep breath and went on breathing! I said, "Surely you know that very soon you can go. But you cannot go before your parents have had time to see you and to say goodbye!" I called the nurse, who couldn't believe her eyes, and she called the doctor. He told me that there really wasn't any hope that Adam would survive and that I should let him go, but I said that Adam had to live until his parents arrived! Surprised, the doctor asked, "Oh, aren't you his mother?" and I said, "No, but his parents are on their way." So the doctor left, shaking his head and telling me that he would stop by later.' When Jeanne and Rex arrived, Adam was breathing as before.

Meanwhile all the people of Daybreak heard the news that Adam was dying, and those in Adam's day programme were gathered in the meeting hall in Daybreak, preparing to come in shifts to bid Adam goodbye. Each person in the programme has severe limitations, so the assistants were discussing who would go first in the wheelchair van and who would wait until 11 a.m. They agreed that Tracy and Michael would go first, so they began to get their coats and wheelchairs, not noticing that Rosie, who was scheduled for a later run, had already toddled out, put her coat half-on, and pushed her wheelchair in front of the entrance to the hall.

Rosie, like Adam, doesn't speak. She learned to walk at the age of 25 after living many years in a crib in a nursing home. Rosie never gets very close to people and she often screams for no apparent reason. She seems to live in a world apart.

When Tracy and Michael were ready to leave, there was Rosie, in her wheelchair, blocking the entrance. Kathy gently lifted her out of it, saying that she would have to wait a bit, but she would be going at 11 a.m. She took her back into the meeting hall, and moved her chair back as well. On her way out the phone rang so she stopped to answer. When she returned two minutes later, who was blocking the entrance, sitting in her wheelchair? Rosie!

Kathy asked her, 'Rosie, are you trying to tell us something?' She waited, and when Kathy went to help her back into the meeting hall, she clung to her chair. 'Maybe you need to go now, but Rosie, you cannot make your loud noises if you go to the hospital! Adam is very, very sick, and we are going to say, "Goodbye." If you start making your loud noises they will ask us all to leave and others won't be allowed to come. What do you think?' Rosie held tight to her chair. It was as if she was saying, 'Please, I want to go, now.'

The nurses, as well as the family, were uncertain

about a parade of people coming into Adam's room to bid him farewell, but for the sake of the people, they allowed it. Rosie, well-warned about her 'noises', was wheeled into the room and up beside Adam's bed. Silently she looked right into Adam's eyes. He appeared to look back. She reached out and took his hand, something that no one had ever seen her do, and she held his hand and looked into his eyes for almost two minutes. Gently she laid his hand back on the bed, and leaned back in her chair, ready to go. Rosie and Adam had said farewell to one another. Rosie was ready to leave.

❦

That morning I received a call in Watertown, Massachusetts, from Kathy Christie, my secretary at Daybreak. She told me that Adam had had a severe setback and that this time there was little hope that he would survive. A few hours later I was on the plane to Toronto.

When I walked into Adam's hospital room, I was deeply moved to see my dear friend lying there, obviously living his final hours with us. I kissed him on the forehead and stroked his hair. Although his eyes were open, I wasn't certain whether he recognised me. Rex, Jeanne, and Ann greeted me, and I was aware of their enormous sadness. They had gone through so much during the last months, and until very recently they had hoped that Adam would pull through again. But now they knew that death was near.

'Thanks, Henri, thanks so much for coming,' Jeanne said to me through her tears. 'You were so close to Adam. I'm afraid his time has come. We're going to have to let him go. He has suffered long enough ... too long.'

Soon after I arrived, Michael, Adam's brother, came with one of the assistants to be with Adam. He headed straight for Adam's bed, talking to himself and to God, saying, 'I ... want ... you to help my brother. Please help my brother walk again.' He looked sadly at his parents, and his father put his arm around him. A few minutes later when Michael saw me, he threw his arms around me, rested his head on my chest, and cried. I held his shaking body for a long time and then turned with him toward Adam on his bed. As Michael held the little container of sacred oil, everyone gathered, and I anointed Adam's forehead and both his hands, asking God to give him all the inner strength he needed to make his final passage.

'My, my, my brother ... is going ... to heaven,' Michael said through his tears. 'My heart is broken. ... My heart is broken, Father.' I held him again, and we cried together. It was heart-rending to witness Michael's sorrow communicated to his parents and the tears that freely flowed as we stood together around Adam. After an hour or so, Michael, with the help of his father, said his goodbye to his brother and left the hospital for his home.

It was now 6 p.m., but Jeanne and Rex continued to follow Adam's every breath behind the oxygen mask, trying to make him as comfortable as possible and calling him to take the next breath. They occasionally moistened his lips with a little sponge. 'He is not giving up easily,' I said. 'He is a real fighter.' Ann Pavilonis said, 'I'm sure he was waiting for Rex, Jeanne, and you to come. Now that you are here and have seen him, it is time to let him go.' Of course, we weren't listening! His parents were trying to encourage him, saying, 'Breathe, Adam! Come on. You can do it! Breathe!' Ann finally called each one of them aside and helped them to see that it was time to stop calling Adam to live. 'You have to bless him and give him permission to go,' she said. Reluctantly, each one came back to Adam and told him that he could now go on. I sat on the bed caressing Adam's head and hair, and once in a while holding his face between my hands.

Members of the Daybreak community continued to come throughout the evening, coming by turn from the waiting room for a short moment to speak their goodbyes to Adam and to talk a little with all of us. Off and on several of us gathered around Adam's bed, held hands, and prayed for him, for his parents and family and his many friends. We asked

God to give us all a deep inner peace and the freedom to let Adam return home when his time had come.

Later that evening the nurse unplugged the monitors and Rex and Ann removed the mask so that Adam could be free from all unnecessary support systems. He was now close to death, and the only thing to do was to make him as comfortable as possible. Then began his struggle to breathe. Although it seemed that he was not feeling any pain, it was strenuous to have to fight for every breath. Jeanne said with a certain pride, 'With such a weak heart, I wonder how he can do it. He certainly doesn't give up easily. He's so strong.' Rex knelt beside the bed and held Adam's hand. Jeanne stood at the other side, her hands on Adam in the bed.

By midnight it seemed that Adam would make it through the night and I began to feel very exhausted. Ann said, 'Go home now and get some sleep. Rex, Jeanne, and I will be here, and we will call you when Adam dies.'

❦

Very soon after I had fallen asleep in my room at the Dayspring, about 1 a.m., Ann called and said, 'Henri, Adam is dead.' I immediately thought of Jesus' words: 'It is fulfilled.' Adam's life – and mission – had come to its end.

Fifteen minutes later I was back at the hospital. Adam lay there, completely still, at peace. No more struggle for the next bit of air, no more fidgeting of his fingers or restless moving of his body. Rex, Jeanne, and Ann were sitting on the bed touching Adam's body. There were tears, tears of loss but also of relief. The four of us held hands, and while looking at Adam's quiet face, we prayed in gratitude for the gift of his 34 years of life, and for all that he had brought to us in his great physical weakness and incredible spiritual strength.

I couldn't stop gazing at his face. I thought, 'Here is the man who more than anyone connected me with my inner self, my community, and my God. Here is the man I was asked to care for, but who took me into his life and into his heart in such an incredibly deep way. Yes, I had cared for him during my first year at Day-break and had come to love him so much, but he has been such an invaluable gift to me. Here is my counsellor, my teacher, and my guide, who could never say a word to me but taught me more than any book, professor, or spiritual director. Here is Adam, my friend, my beloved friend, the most vulnerable person I have ever known and at the same time the most powerful. He is dead now. His life is over. His task is accomplished. He has returned to the heart of God from which he came.'

I felt an immense sadness but also an immense gladness. I had lost a companion and gained a guardian for the rest of my life. I prayed, 'May all the angels guide Adam now into paradise and welcome him home to the loving embrace of his God.'

Death is such a mystery, forcing us to ask ourselves, 'Why do I live? How do I live? For whom do I live?' And also, 'Am I prepared to die . . . now . . . later?' It was as if Adam gave me the freedom to let these questions emerge within me. It was as if he said, 'Don't be afraid, Henri. Let my death help you to befriend yours. When you are no longer afraid of your own death, then you can live fully, freely, and joyfully.'

What a privilege it was to be there with Rex, Jeanne, and Ann, and to experience with them this sacred moment of passage. I felt like John, the beloved disciple of Jesus, who stood with Mary under the cross. I don't have any biological children, but Adam had become like a son. He had also become like a father. Here in front of his still body I knew that God had not left me alone, childless, or homeless.

When Jesus was dying he said to Mary, looking at his beloved disciple, 'Mother, this is your son', and to John, 'This is your mother', thus making his death the beginning of a new communion. Adam too, at that moment and in the days following, forged the bonds of communion between his family, past and present community members, and friends.

Around 3 a.m. the doctor came. Rex and Jeanne realised that the time for their first farewell had come. Rex said, 'Please, doctor, be gentle with his body.' That was what he had been for 34 years.

When we left the hospital Rex and Jeanne insisted on taking me home. It was very, very cold. Everything was still, covered with the snow from the seventh snowstorm of that hard winter. Fifteen minutes later they dropped me off at the Dayspring. As I waved goodbye to them, I tried to imagine what was going on in their hearts. A man and a woman, driving through the night grieving for their beloved son, to whom they had given all their love and care. I could hardly grasp their anguish. At the same time I was convinced that Adam was near, protecting them and watching over them. He would not leave them alone in their grief.

❦

CHAPTER SEVEN

Adam's Wake and Burial

WHEN I WOKE UP the next morning I realised that I needed to spend some special time with Adam's brother, Michael. Mary Bastedo, who is responsible for the home where Michael lives, suggested that I take him out for a Coke. 'He really wants to be with you right now,' she said. So Michael and I made a little trip to a restaurant in Richmond Hill and had our Coke and coffee. We sat there talking about each other and Adam. I said, 'Michael, I am so glad we are friends.' In his characteristic way Michael grabbed the armrest of his chair, moved a little closer to me, smiled, and answered, 'Yes . . . Father. I am . . . your . . . friend.'

I said, 'Your brother Adam is gone now and is with God. Today we will go to the funeral home and you will see his body, and tomorrow we will bury his body in the cemetery.' Michael looked at me with tears in his eyes and said, 'I don't like that, Father. I . . . don't like that . . . in the . . . ground,' and he pointed to the floor. I said, 'I don't like it either, Mike. But I really hope that God is going to give Adam a new body, so that he can walk all around in heaven and speak, and talk with his grandpa and grandma and his uncle, who are already there.'

Michael's grief was deep. But happily from time to time he could be distracted for a short moment. One small diversion I could offer him was to let him sit in my car, turn on the radio, and enjoy a ride. I sensed that Michael would be all right. He is a very prayerful man, and I felt that his faith would help him in the days to come.

That afternoon when I went to the funeral home and saw Adam lying in his coffin, I was very surprised. He looked so young, like an 18-year-old who had just fallen asleep. His face was very gentle. His skin was soft. His hair was neatly combed. He wore a wonderful shirt and a pale yellow woollen sweater. His beauty and youthfulness brought tears to my eyes. It was the first time I had seen him with his mouth closed and very, very still. It was hard for me to believe that this man had given me so much and at the same time had never spoken a word to me, never been able to run in the garden, play ball, go regularly to school, or read books. He just liked to hang out together in the company of his friends! Here he looked so healthy, so whole, so handsome that I couldn't keep my eyes off him. It was as if he was already giving me a glimpse of the new body he would have in the resurrection.

Jeanne had wondered whether it would be good to have an open coffin. 'Adam is dead now,' she had mused. 'Why should people's last impression of him be that of his dead body?' Nevertheless I had asked her to consider leaving the coffin open for a while so that those who really wanted to see him before his burial could do so. When Jeanne saw her son, so gentle, so handsome, and so peaceful, she realised how good it was for us to be able to look at him, stroke his hair, and kiss his forehead.

During the afternoon and evening visiting hours, most of the Daybreak community came to be with Adam one more time. The largest room in the funeral parlour was crowded with people. Ann, John David, Leszek, Jody, and Claudia, the assistants who had lived with Adam in the New House – for months or for years – were overcome with pain as they realised that Adam was really gone. It was hard for them to imagine how life could go on in the house without him.

And then there were Adam's friends and house-mates. John came, even though he is terribly afraid of hospitals, funeral homes, churches, and cemeteries since they all make him think of the death of his mother. John had lived with Adam from the day Adam came to Daybreak and had always shown him much affection and love. He kept repeating the phrases he knows best, like 'Henri, are you home tonight?' He wanted contact, presence, closeness, but his own experience and wounds didn't allow him to give expression to his anguished heart.

Rosie also came. Rosie arrived at Daybreak in the same year as Adam. Although she is profoundly disabled and to outsiders she seems to live in her own impenetrable world, those who lived and worked with her noticed how deeply Adam's illness and death had touched her. Having had her goodbye time, Rosie was content to toddle about the room, go up with an assistant and look at Adam, then sit for a while on the floor away from the crowd. Often Rosie expresses her joy or pain with a loud, piercing sound, but here, for the most part, she was still and focused as she looked at her friend, feeling deeply the grief of his leaving.

Michael, not Adam's brother, came too in his wheelchair. Because of his severe cerebral palsy and mental handicap, it is extremely hard for Michael to let anyone know what goes on within him. Even there, looking at Adam's still body, Michael was unable to express himself, but his presence in front of Adam evoked deep emotions in all who stood around. It was only the next day at the funeral that his voice rose in anguish with a piercing cry.

Roy, Adam's other housemate, cannot face death directly. He decided that coming to the funeral home would be too disturbing for him. But at home he kept saying, 'How is Adam? How is Adam?' He was trying to remain joyful and optimistic in the midst of his grief. At the same time he was suffering deep down, and he was unable to control the sudden out-bursts of frustration and anger. He deeply loved Adam and always spoke fondly to him. There was a real connection between these two men. After the funeral, Ann and Roy visited Adam's grave together. Roy seemed to feel better after that.

The room where Adam's body was laid out was filled with people, not only members of the com-munity and family, but also old friends from far away. Greg and his wife, Eileen, who had met in the New House and had lived with Adam, drove back from Chicago; Steve, who had grown close to Adam while being an assistant in the home and at Adam's day programme, flew in from Seattle; and Peter, who had accompanied Adam for two years as head of the New House, flew from Nova Scotia to be present at the wake and funeral.

Several times during visiting hours we stopped talking and formed a large circle around the coffin to pray and to share. I read the twenty-seventh Psalm, feeling as though it was giving a voice to Adam. After the time of prayer we kept standing in the circle, and several people told stories about Adam, dreams or events that evoked a smile or a tear, or both. Sorrow and joy kept dancing together around Adam's body. Grief and laughter, a sense of irretrievable loss and a sense of immense gain. It was as if we could hear Adam say to us what Jesus said to the grieving disciples: 'Was it not necessary that the Christ should suffer before entering into his glory?' (Luke 24:26).

Jesus said other things to offer us hope at this moment. He said,

> Unless a wheat grain falls into the earth and dies,
> it remains only a single grain;
> but if it dies
> it yields a rich harvest.
> Anyone who loves life loses it;
> anyone who hates life in this world
> will keep it for eternal life. (John 12:24–25)

As we all stood around Adam's body I felt that Jesus' words about himself gave us a glimpse into the mystery of the immense fruitfulness not only of Adam's life but of his death as well.

On Thursday, 15 February 1996, a few hundred people gathered in St Mary Immaculate Catholic Church in Richmond Hill to celebrate Adam's life and death. As Adam's body was brought into the church and everyone rose to welcome him, I was overcome by the realisation that all these men and women had been deeply touched by this most vulnerable and beautiful young man. This was not a brilliant artist, a famous musician, a great religious figure, or a successful political leader. No, this was Adam, who spoke to us, not in words but by his example; Adam, who never needed to travel, give speeches, or write books to deliver his message of peace. This was Adam, who had never even had to earn a dime because he called a community of care to form around him; Adam, for whom we all rose with tears in our eyes, and for whom our hearts were full of love.

As eight of Adam's close friends accompanied the coffin to the front of the church, we sang:

> Blest are they, the poor in spirit,
> Theirs is the Kingdom of God.
> Blest are they, full of sorrow,
> They shall be consoled.

We listened to Paul's words, 'God chose those who by human standards are weak to shame the strong' (1 Cor. 1:27).

And we listened to the words expressing Jesus' vision: 'Blessed are the gentle: they shall inherit the earth' (Matt. 5:4). We realised that indeed these words were about Adam.

Standing in front of Adam's body, holding the eucharistic bread and speaking Jesus' words, 'Take and eat, this is my Body given for you', I knew in a whole new way that God has become body for us so that we can touch God and be healed. God's body and Adam's body are one, because, Jesus tells us clearly, 'Insofar as you did this to one of the least of these brothers of mine, you did it to me' (Matt.

25:40). In Adam, indeed, we touched the living
Christ among us.

Everyone came to the front of the church to receive
the Body of Christ, and – after the Eucharist –
everyone came again to touch Adam's coffin as a last
farewell. As we let our hands stroke the wood, we
sang the old Irish blessing:

> May the road rise with you.
> May the wind be always at your back.
> May the sun shine warm upon your face.
> May the rain fall softly upon your fields.
> Until we meet again,
> may God hold you in the hollow of God's hand.

Then those who had accompanied Adam's body to
the altar led him out of the church while we sang:

> God will raise you up on eagle's wings,
> bear you on the breath of the dawn,
> make sure you shine like the sun,
> and hold you in the palm of God's hand.

❦

Michael and I joined the lead car in the procession
to the cemetery. Just after the service Jeanne had
said to me, 'Michael is in such grief. I wonder if it's
good for him to go to the cemetery.' But I sensed
that Michael wanted to be close to his family and
friends, and that it would be okay for him to live his

grief to the end. I said to him, 'Why don't you come with me in the lead car?' And Michael immediately responded, 'Yes . . . Father. I will go . . . with you . . . in your car.'

At the cemetery the pallbearers carried Adam's body to the burial site and placed it on the metal structure on which it could be lowered into the grave. The grave itself was covered with large wooden planks, and the heap of earth beside the grave was shielded with large sheets of artificial grass. At least a hundred people had accompanied Adam's body to his resting place.

It was a beautiful day, very cold, but the sun was casting its bright light over the snow-white cemetery. There was no wind, and every spoken word could be clearly heard.

Michael had shown great interest in the holy-water sprinkler I was carrying, and I felt that he was the one who should bless Adam's grave and coffin with holy water. After a short prayer, I gave Michael the sprinkler, and, while I held him tightly, he bent over the coffin and carefully blessed it, slowly walking from one side to the other. Then I prayed:

> Dear God, into your hands we commend our son, brother, and friend Adam. We are confident that with all who have lived and died in Christ he will be raised to life on the last day and live with You forever.

Welcome our dear Adam into Paradise, and help us to comfort each other with the assurance of our faith until we all meet in Christ, to be with You and with Adam forever.

After these prayers two young men in overalls and with hard hats appeared. They immediately started to remove the artificial grass and the large planks underneath the casket. I had to smile. They made me think of the gravediggers who appear in Shakespeare's *Hamlet* to offer a little comic relief. While all of us waited, their youthful energy and busyness made it clear that indeed we were going to bury Adam and not leave him alone above the ground in the cold snow. When all the planks had been removed, the two men let the coffin descend into the grave. It felt like a long, slow journey into the earth. As it was lowered we sang, 'Alleluia, Alleluia, Alleluia.' The two men kept looking deep into the hole until the coffin touched the ground, and the ropes and the metal lift could be taken away. Then they handed Rex and me large shovels with which we dug into the fresh earth, letting it fall with resounding thuds onto the coffin below. The shovels then went from hand to hand until all who wished had had a turn.

This was so final. I looked at Adam's coffin deep in the grave with one simple bouquet of flowers on top of it, and I knew without a doubt that Adam would never be with us again. Loads of soil would cover his body, and gradually it would become part of the earth surrounding it. It was in front of that big hole that I was confronted with the finality of death as well as with hope in the resurrection.

We all felt it. We dropped the frozen clumps of earth into the grave, and heard the dull noise on the coffin, our grieving hearts torn. Michael started to sob in the arms of his friends, and John, finally able to let his sorrow be known, erupted in loud howls of grief. At that moment we knew the depth of our powerlessness and loneliness. The sun, the snow, the bitter cold, the grave, the crying, and Adam's body down in the ground they told us about our unspeakable sorrow. When we had all had our turn with the shovels, we sang again the Irish blessing we had sung in the church, and I said, 'Let's now go in peace.' Slowly the crowd turned and began to depart.

I lingered a while with some others. It was hard to leave this lovely man all alone there. I took my last look at the snow-covered place where Adam's body lay, and I felt his newfound solitude. Adam is dead. He will not come back. We will never touch him again. We will have to go on without his physical presence among us. How? We don't know. We just have to wait, to feel the pain, to mourn the loss, to let our tears come. Adam has left us. He is at peace, and we have to continue living with hope. One thing I know clearly. We have to stay together, trusting that he who brought us together desires us to stay together. As we drove to the place where we all would have lunch I knew that Adam would be glad to see us there, with many tears and occasional smiles.

CHAPTER EIGHT

Adam's Resurrection

ADAM'S RESURRECTION began in the grief of those who loved him. And that grief was very real and deep. After the burial, when we all came together in the large meeting hall of the Daybreak community, I realised how great our loss was. Not just for me, but for many people Adam was the soul of the community, the still centre around which we lived our restless lives. Now that centre was gone.

What now? What next? How would we go on? Could we go on? During the days of Adam's wake and burial there was still a sense of his presence. We could still look at his youthful face and touch him. Now there was only emptiness, absence. I kept wondering how Jesus' friends must have felt after his burial. Numb? Confused? Angry? Bitter? The bottom of their existence had fallen out! The meaning of their lives had been taken away! Everything had come to a complete standstill. No more teaching and preaching, no common meals and shared moments of prayer and quiet, no more intimate times of conversation. Where were the crowds, the miracles, the great expectation of a new order, of true freedom? Where was the abundance of fish and bread and the pure joy of living? A large stone had been rolled across the entrance of the tomb (Matt. 27:60), and seals had been put on the stone (Matt. 27:66). The finality of it all was so shocking. What was there to do but go home or just sit in pure bewilderment?

We cannot speak or even think about resurrection without entering into the depth of our grief. Neither Jesus' friends nor the friends of Adam could say, 'Don't cry, he will return.' We needed to cry, to feel his loss, to mourn his passing. Grief is emptiness, darkness, meaninglessness, uselessness, paralysis. Even more it is a gradual dying within us of the loved one who had found a dwelling place in our hearts. Grief is a departing hour by hour, day by day, minute by minute. For a long time we think or act as if he is still there, but at every turn we realise he is gone, for all time. Who is getting Adam up this morning? But . . . he is no longer here! Who will give him his bath, shave him, comb his hair, and put on his new jacket? But . . . he is no longer here! Who will prepare his breakfast, help him with his orange juice, and get him ready for the day? But . . . he is no longer here! Tonight Rex and Jeanne will come . . . but to be with us, not with Adam. It is an ongoing dying, a being surprised again and again by his absence, a slow, painful leaving, a wrenching loneliness. We cannot

circumvent our grief. We cannot shorten it. We have
to give it time, much time.

❦

Where then does the resurrection begin? When would
we see Adam again? When would we dare to speak
not only about his absence but about his presence as
well? For us the resurrection started in visions and
dreams.

Yvonne, Adam's good friend, told a story that she
imagined, right in the midst of her grief. She was
thinking about Adam, about his death, and about
their friendship. She became conscious that the next
time she would see Adam would be in heaven. Then
she imagined that she was walking into heaven. As
she walked she saw a radiant-looking young man
approaching her. She was puzzled because she did not
recognise him but he came right up to her and spoke.
'Hi, Yvonne,' he said. 'You don't recognise me, do
you?' Yvonne kept looking at him feeling she knew
him but not knowing how. Then he laughed and
said, 'I'm Adam. Your friend. Do you remember me?'
Yvonne was consoled by his youthful energy and
welcome.

Elizabeth, a longtime member of L'Arche, had a
dream. She told us, 'In my dream I saw Adam
running and dancing, jumping up and down, free as
a bird. I saw him as a free spirit, laughing and talking
and moving his head, arms, and legs like a beautiful

athlete. He was so jubilant, so radiant, doing all the things he had never been able to do while he was with us. When I woke up I was thrilled to have seen Adam dancing!'

I myself didn't have any vision or dream. On the contrary, I had this strange feeling in my stomach that nothing was worthwhile anymore. That feeling was not there all the time – I kept on with my routines – but once in a while I said to myself, 'Why do I do all of this? Why should I visit another person, eat another meal, write another book, celebrate another liturgy? It all comes to nothing anyhow. Why love when all ends in death?' I felt a draining fatigue as I lay down on my bed and I asked myself, 'Why should I get up again?'

But every time I spoke about Adam to my friends, they listened. And they listened in a different way than when they listened to my other words. They listened to my grieving heart and heard there the voice of that silent young man I had loved so much. And as I talked they said, 'You really loved him, didn't you? Tell us more.' And I did tell them more – about Adam's birth, his wonderful parents, his coming to Daybreak, our relationship and how he touched my heart. Such a simple story. But every time I told it I could see new life and new hope emerging in the hearts of my listening friends. My grief became their joy, my loss was their gain, and my dying their coming to new life. Very slowly I started to see Adam coming alive in the hearts of those who had never known him, as if they were being made part of a great mystery. Then someone said, 'Maybe you should write about Adam, so that many people can know his story and rejoice in it.'

❦

Is this when his resurrection began, in the midst of my grief? That is what happened to the mourning Mary of Magdala when she heard a familiar voice calling her by her name. That is what happened for the downcast disciples on the road to Emmaus when a stranger talked to them on the road and their hearts burned within them. It happened for the fearful disciples in the upper room when they heard, 'Peace be with you!' and loving words of forgiveness. It happened for the grieving friends of Jesus who went back to fishing in the lake and filled their boat after a man on the shore told them to throw out their nets to starboard, and later invited them to break their fast with him.

Mourning turns to dancing, grief turns to joy, despair turns to hope, and fear turns to love. Then hesitantly someone is saying, 'He is risen, he is risen indeed.'

My heart refuses to believe that all Adam lived in his body was for nothing. His incredible vulnerability and life, which became the mysterious gateway through which he poured out his love to so many people, are destined for glory. Just as the wounds of Jesus in his risen body were the signs that allowed others to recognise him, Adam's wounds become marks of his unique presence in our midst. Adam's broken body was the seed of his new, risen life. Paul says:

> Someone may ask: How are dead people raised, and what sort of body do they have when they come? How foolish! What you sow must die before it is given new life; and what you sow is not the body that is to be, but only a bare grain, of wheat I dare say, or some other kind; it is God who gives it the sort of body that he has chosen for it, and for each kind of seed its own kind of body. (1 Cor. 15:35–38)

Adam's unique body is the seed of his resurrected life. When I saw his youthful beauty in the coffin I had a glimpse of this new life. I have to trust the visions and dreams of my friends and the new hope that emerges in the hearts of those I tell about Adam's life. I have to trust in what happens through my own and other people's grief. And as I trust I must believe that I will see that the resurrection of Adam, the beloved son of God, is not only something to wait for but also something that is already happening in the midst of our grief.

CHAPTER NINE

❦

Adam's Spirit

A DAM, WHO CAME from God and was sent for 34 years into this world, has returned to God. His mission is fulfilled. Yet it is not over. It will never be over, because love is stronger than fear and life is stronger than death. Adam's love and Adam's life are not meant for corruption. They are eternal, because they are part of God's love and God's life. Just before his death Jesus said:

> 'I am telling you the truth: it is for your own good that I am going, because unless I go, the Holy Spirit will not come to you, but if I go, I will send him to you . . . [and] he will lead you to the complete truth.' (John 16:6–7, 13)

The spirit of Adam is the Spirit of Jesus. It is the Spirit of 'love, joy, peace, patience, kindness, goodness, truthfulness, gentleness and self-control' (Gal. 5:22). Everyone who lived with Adam has been touched by his beautiful spirit. It is the Spirit that healed so many and brought so many a new understanding of their lives. Adam's death did not extinguish his Spirit. On the contrary, death released his spirit to blow wherever, and to touch people who never met Adam but who hear about him through those who had the privilege of knowing him. Therefore, keeping the memory of Adam alive is much more than keeping his picture on the wall, mentioning him in our prayers, or having a special service on the anniversary of his death. Keeping his memory alive means remaining open to receive the Spirit of Jesus that lived in him and is now being sent to us. There is still so much for Adam to give us. And we so much need what he has to give!

A few weeks ago I went for a short visit to the New House. Everyone was there – Rosie, Roy, John, Michael, Ann, and others. Adam was not there. But we talked about him. John David said, 'With Adam gone, things are different. We feel his absence every moment.' Jody added, 'We miss him so much.' And Leszek simply said, 'Can I bring you something to drink?'

We stood and sat in different parts of the living room. Not a closed circle but a broken circle, a circle of grief and pain. There was a deep sense that we were at the end of an era. Our community is 26 years old, and for 11 of those years Adam had been there weaving his unique shape and style into its fabric. We all felt that Adam's death marked the end of our youth as a community. Our grief was moving us into adulthood as a body of friends. We had seen people come and go, people start a new life here, live fully, and then die. We now had a long history together and we could remember our past. Adam's death left us waiting for something new, something we had no words for yet.

Our conversation gradually shifted from Adam to our own lives and futures. John David was preparing for his forthcoming marriage with Sheilagh, and Jody for her wedding with David. Leszek was getting ready to return home to Poland to continue his studies, and Petro, a Ukrainian assistant, was applying to the seminary in Lvov. I realised that Adam's assistants were going out all over the world to continue their lives.

Adam's spirit will be with them in their hearts. Wherever they live or work he will continue to remind them of the many things he taught them. And what wasn't so clear when they lived their busy lives with him will become clear as they remember him in the years ahead. They will say to their friends, 'Let me tell you about Adam, with whom I lived in the New House at Daybreak, many years ago.' And as they tell the story they will discover again that Adam's spirit, the spirit of love, will continue to bear fruit in their lives. He will keep guiding them as they fulfil their own missions.

Meanwhile those who stay – John, Rosie, Roy, Michael, Ann, and others – still point to the empty chair and to Adam's picture on the wall. They will tell those who come for dinner, 'Adam lived here. He was a wonderful friend and guide. Because of Adam's life and death we have been gifted with peace, hope, love, and immense gratitude.'

Conclusion

A DAM'S LIFE and our relationship have been such true and lasting gifts to me. From a worldly perspective telling about our relationship makes no sense at all. But I, Henri, Adam's friend, decided to write it down. I didn't embellish it. I didn't soften or sweeten it. I tried to write it as simply and directly as I could. I am a witness of Adam's truth. I know that I couldn't have told Adam's story if I hadn't first known Jesus' story. Jesus' story gave me eyes to see and ears to hear the story of Adam's life and death. It was in the light of that story that I felt compelled to write about Adam's story as simply and directly as I could.

L'Arche became my community and Daybreak my home because of Adam – because of holding Adam in my arms and touching him in complete purity and complete freedom. Adam gave me a sense of belonging. He rooted me in the truth of my physical being, anchored me in my community, and gave me a deep experience of God's presence in our life together. Without having touched Adam, I don't know where I would be today. Those first 14 months at Daybreak, washing, feeding, and just sitting with Adam, gave me the home I had been yearning for; not just a home with good people but a home in my own body, in the body of my community, in the body of the church, yes, in the body of God.

I have heard about and read about the life of Jesus, but I was never able to touch or see him. I was able to touch Adam. I saw him and I touched his life. I physically touched him when I gave him a bath, shaved him, and brushed his teeth. I touched him when I carefully dressed him, walked him to the breakfast table, and helped him to bring the spoon to his mouth. Others touched him when they gave him a massage, did exercises with him, and sat with him in the swimming pool and Jacuzzi. His parents touched him. Murray, Cathy, and Bruno touched him. That's what we did: touched Adam! And what is said of Jesus must be said of Adam: 'Everyone who touched him was healed' (Mark 6:56). Each of us who has touched Adam has been made whole somewhere; it has been our common experience.

Thus, Adam's story becomes an expression of my belief, my creed, and also an expression of my own story with all my strengths and disabilities. As I wrote this book I realised increasingly that every word involved me as much as it did Adam. It can't be otherwise! It was my love for Adam that made me want to write his story in the first place because it was a love turned to grief, soaked in tears, and full of longing. Right there, where love and sorrow met in my heart, God's Spirit inspired me, saying: 'Sit down. Write. Tell the story. You can do it not only because you loved Adam but because you know that other story so well.'

So I sat down – in the midst of my grief – and I wrote and wrote and wrote. Words came easily because as I wrote I saw ever more clearly that Adam had lived the story of Jesus that I have been telling every day to anyone who wanted to hear it.

Now I rest for a while. The story is told. I hope and pray that many will read it and understand.